Country Wines
— and Cordials —

Country Wines
—— and Cordials ——

MARSHALL CAVENDISH EDITIONS

Consultant editor: B.C.A. Turner

Executive editor: Isabel Moore

Contributing editor: Jeanette Dixon

House editors: Renny Harrop
              Eden Phillips

Designer: Mike Rose

Photography: Roger Phillips

Picture credits: Mary Evans Picture Library 11, 13, 14/5, 119.
                Michael Holford   8, 10.
                Mansell Collection   9(t), 12, 16, 115.
                Ann Ronan Picture Library 9(b), 17.

Illustrations: Ian Beck
               Rod Shone
               Lucy Su

Published by
Marshall Cavendish Editions, a division of
Marshall Cavendish Books Limited
58 Old Compton Street
London W1V 5PA

First printing 1980

ISBN 0 85685 856 0

Printed in Great Britain

Foreword

Wine means different things to different people. To some it suggests a visit to a vineyard or sampling the world's great vintages as a complement to fine food; to others, a supermarket purchase or taking a bottle to a party. But, whatever one's expectation of a glass of wine, the ideal is surely a clear, richly coloured, fine flavoured aromatic drink arriving in the glass as inexpensively as possible. If, allied to this utopian pleasure, you can produce the nectar at home, what could be more satisfying? Alas, too often home-made wine is a substance no more palatable or interesting than a tin of concentrate from the chemist fermenting forlornly in a plastic dustbin. *Country Wines and Cordials* suggests a myriad of alternatives to this dismal prospect, using natural ingredients and time-honoured methods.

The making of wine has ever attracted the eccentric, but here you will not find ingredients as natural or recipes as time-honoured as those recommended by Apicius in his First Century Roman Cookbook. His list of necessities for concocting the perfect spiced wine ends with such items as "6 scruples each of mastic,

aromatic leaves and costmary, 3 scruples of saffron and 18 pints of the proper kind of wine", and the conclusion that "As it should already be bitter you need not add coal". Nevertheless, there follow wine, beer and ale recipes handed down through generations which use many equally unlikely basics. Most of these are easy to come by in town or country.

Country Wines and Cordials does not assume a specialized knowledge of the world of home-brewing, although many an 'expert' will find new ideas to stimulate his enthusiasm and taste buds. It is a world rich in legend and history, and here are offered speculations on the origins of the 'honeymoon' and 'taking a man down a peg or two', as well as the story of the first recorded hangover. Alongside the romantic myths of wine, there is a wealth of practical information on equipment, timing, bottling, corking, and, of course, drinking the stuff! According to the author and critic George Saintsbury, "It is the testimony of all history that alcoholic liquors have been used by the strongest, wisest, handsomest, and in every way the best races of all times". Welcome to their company.

Contents

Introduction

An Assyrian representation of 668–627 BC, showing Ashurbanipal and his wife feasting in a garden. Wine appears to form the major part of the feast.

Man has been making alcoholic drinks for a very long time. Precisely how and when the pleasing effects of alcohol were first discovered we cannot be sure, but almost certainly the discovery came about by happy accident: honey, fruit juice, the sap in the hollow of a tree would all, if left for long enough at the right temperature, ferment spontaneously and cause a feeling of well-being in whoever drank them. According to a Persian legend, we can thank (or blame) a woman for the discovery of alcohol. One day Jamshid, a mythological king, opened one of the jars in which his grapes were stored to find that they had changed into a pungent purple liquid. Unwilling to risk any ill effects he had the jar marked 'poison' and sent to the cellar. There it remained until a neglected and lonely courtesan found it and, deciding to end her life, drank its contents. To her surprise, she awoke from the deep sleep the 'poison' had induced feeling much more cheerful, and so she hurried to the king to tell him of her amazing discovery. From then on, many jars of grapes were left to ferment!

However the discovery was made, once alcohol became available it was treasured. Regarded as a gift from the gods it was offered back to them in sacrifices, and the mythologies of most countries include accounts of the gods' feasting and drinking. As a tribute to the king, a gift of hospitality, or an item of diet necessary for health and vigour, alcohol quickly became an essential feature of daily life and as long ago as the second millennium B.C., its potential as a source of revenue was recognized by Hammurabi's government in Babylon.

The first fermented drinks probably tasted dreadful—it was their effect rather than their flavour which held the attraction. The crude flavour of the alcohol had to be disguised by spicing the drinks heavily and making them very sweet. Of the beverages which have come down to us today, mead (made from a solution of fermented honey and water) is undoubtedly the oldest and was probably being drunk as long ago as 12,000 B.C. Perhaps the knowledge of how to make mead led to the fermenting of sweet grape juice and hence to wine. Certainly

8

by 6000 B.C. the ancient Persians were growing vines for the purpose of making wine and it is possible that their cereal crops—early forms of wheat and barley—were also used as a base for ales and beers.

As the Persian Empire expanded, the knowledge of how to make many of these fermented drinks spread and eventually reached Egypt. Two forms of ale were certainly made by the Egyptians—one, rather weak, was drunk mainly by the workers while it was still fermenting; the other, a matured ale, was reserved for the wealthier classes (who obviously attached great importance to its brightness as it was artificially clarified with a type of fuller's earth). Ale was, however, generally regarded as

Treading grapes was not for the Egyptians!

inferior—wine was the drink the Egyptians offered to their gods and left in the tombs of their dead. It was also the drink of hospitality: many Egyptian tomb paintings depict banquets at which guests appear to be greatly enjoying wine (sometimes to excess!). Indeed, the Egyptians became highly skilled in the making of wine, leaving it to mature in jars inscribed with the name and year of the vintage.

The Greek merchants who traded with Egypt tasted wine when they came in search of

Dionysus, celebrated by the Greeks as god of wine.

trade, and soon the vine was taken to Athens and other Greek cities. There it flourished and before long assumed a place alongside olive oil and wheat as a major commodity of trade. It also became an essential part of Greek religious festivals: after the grape harvest there were ceremonies of thanksgiving during which libations of wine were poured over the earth as an offering to Dionysus, the god of wine. In general, the Greeks were moderate in their drinking habits and drank their wine mixed with water—undiluted wine was considered fit only for barbarians! As in Egypt, wine and food were the traditional gifts of hospitality, and wine was also used for medicinal purposes mixed with extracts of herbs, flowers and roots. To give some of their wines more interest, the Greeks added pine needles and created retsina, a very distinctive wine which survives to this day.

With the decline of Greek civilization, the Roman Empire assumed domination of the known world; Dionysus became Bacchus—and wine drinking continued. The Romans, unfortunately, do not seem to have been so abstemious as the Greeks, and many a tale of Bacchic revelries gradually degenerating into orgies of drunkenness, gluttony and fornication were recorded. Despite the excesses of the later Empire, however, the Romans brought relative peace to the countries they conquered, and also the vine. And with peace, the techniques of vine-growing improved. Certainly wine was held in high regard, and Roman literature contains many references to the pleasure that drinking can bring.

They were not so impressed with the ale they found being made and drunk by the Celtic peoples they conquered, particularly the British—the Emperor Julian was particularly damning:

An amphora. Traditionally a two-handed vessel, the amphora was in common use by both Greeks and Romans. This particular example shows a typical scene of feasting.

On Wine Made from Barley
Who made you and from what
By the true Bacchus I know not
He smells of nectar
But you smell of goat.

The Celtic ale in question was probably made from wheat or barley, sometimes flavoured with nettles, yarrow or other herbs, but often drunk unflavoured, so one can understand the Roman lack of enthusiasm. The Romans, or at least the officers among them, continued to drink imported wine, as did the native merchants and chieftains. For everyone else, however, ale was the everyday drink and mead the one for festive occasions. Athenaeus, an Egyptian commenting on English drinking habits around A.D. 200 tells us: 'The rich drink wine from Italy or from around Marseilles. Poorer classes drink beer made from wheat and prepared with honey'. This was to be the pattern for the next thousand years.

From Bacchus to Beer

The withdrawal of the Romans from Britain and the arrival of the hard-drinking Norsemen, Angles and Saxons brought ale into even greater prominence. Drinking contests were popular among young warriors. Long cattle horns (the forerunners of the traditional 'Yards of Ale') would be filled with ale and competitors would attempt to drain them in one continuous swallow, without pause. Pegs were inserted into the competition horns and a challenger might succeed in drinking a peg or two more than the champion—or 'taking him down a peg or two'.

Ale, then, was the drink of everyman and everyday (and was brewed by every family); but along with this widespread consumption of alcohol went growing abuse of it. There were, of course, very sound reasons for drinking ale: from the health point of view, water supplies were at best unreliable and at worst downright unsanitary. The only drawback was that the alcohol which made the beer safe also tended to loosen tongues and remove inhibitions. Many writings and records dating between the ninth and twelfth centuries refer to drunkenness. Edicts and decrees setting out penalties for both monk and layman issued forth from local kings and bishops; ale houses were limited to one per village; attempts were made to standardize serving vessels; and prices were prescribed. By and large, however, drunkenness was looked upon with a certain amount of tolerance, it was such a prevalent vice.

The Norman Conquest did little to affect brewing. There are references in the *Domesday Book* to 'cerevissarii'—the term seems to have been used loosely to mean either a servant who brewed ale for his master or a peasant who paid part of his rent in ale. (In wine-growing areas of Europe it was common for peasants to pay part of their rent in wine.) Although we know little about brewing techniques in this period, the quality of the ale does seem to have improved dramatically from that which the Emperor Julian had derided in the fourth century. By 1158, at any rate, King Henry II of England seems to have thought quite well of it. Anxious to obtain a French bride for his son Prince Henry, he sent his chancellor, Becket, to France to demand a suitable princess. The entourage was of immense grandeur and magnificence, designed to give an impression of luxury and great wealth, as befitted the king and his court. In the great procession were two splendid chariots, each drawn by five noble horses. They were filled to capacity with iron-bound barrels of ale, a gift to the French people. William Fitzstephen, Becket's chaplain, reported that the French marvelled at: 'A drink most wholesome, clear of all dregs, rivalling wine in colour and surpassing it in flavour.'

In 1188 ale became subject to taxation. Henry II needed money for the Crusade against Saladin and introduced a tax on 'moveables' which became known as the Saladin tithe; one-tenth of the stock of every brewer was required. A similar levy of one-fifteenth of the stock was made in 1228 and another of one-fortieth in 1488, and so it has continued down through the centuries.

At least two different kinds of ale were on sale in medieval times and the price was regulated by the Assize of Bread and Ale. The law dictated that a gallon of one type of ale was to be sold for three farthings and the other for a penny. The ale could only be sold by the gallon, the half-gallon or the quarter-gallon in vessels marked by the seal of the alderman. But there was no means of controlling the quality and so eventually the post of official ale-conner or taster was created. His duty was to visit ale houses proclaiming by a stake outside that newly brewed beer was available. He would purchase a quart of the new ale, pour some on a wooden bench and sit in the pool in his leather breeches for half an hour without altering his position. In the meantime he drank the rest of the ale and chatted to the customers. At the end of his stay he would attempt to stand up. If his breeches stuck to the bench then the ale was deemed to be of poor quality, containing unfermented sugar; if they did not then it was

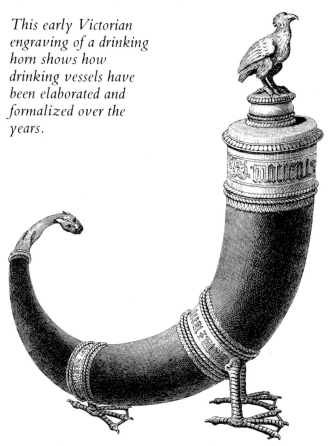

This early Victorian engraving of a drinking horn shows how drinking vessels have been elaborated and formalized over the years.

considered to be of good quality.

The post of ale-conner was to last for centuries and, not long after the first appearance of this worthy gentleman, another innovation was made which was to have much farther-reaching effects on traditional methods of brewing in Britain. Around 1400 a strange Dutch ale flavoured with hops was imported into a small corner of the south coast of England. Strongly resisted for many years, hopped ale would eventually usurp traditional ale as the country's national drink—beer.

Not only ale

There was such an abundance of wine and strong drink, of pyment and claret, of new wine and mead and mulberry wine and all intoxicating liquors in so much abundance that even ale which the Engl-

ish brew excellently, especially in Kent, found no place; but rather ale stood so low in this matter as the pot-herbs among other dishes.

So Geraldus Cambrinser described a meal he had with the monks at Canterbury in the latter part of the twelfth century. Ale was by no means the only drink to be enjoyed by the English during the Middle Ages; cider and mead were always highly regarded and were made in many homes. The Celts had experimented with their meads, adding fruit juices, herbs and spices and had produced a varied range of drinks as a result: 'metheglin' (the correct term for a mead containing spices) is a Celtic word. At feasts and weddings mead was particularly popular. Indeed, to celebrate a marriage, relatives and friends used to drink mead with the happy couple for the 28 days following their wedding. Could this be the origin of the 'honeymoon'?

With the marriage of Henry II to Eleanor of

An occupational hazard of the home-brewer!

Aquitaine in 1152, England inherited all the great wine-producing land around Bordeaux, and great quantities of wine began to be imported. For the first time, grape wine became freely available and was widely on sale in taverns and inns. It was, of course, more expensive than ale, selling at three pence rather than a penny a gallon.

To what extent wine was made from native fruits and flowers is very difficult to establish. There are references to 'apple wine' but this could well mean cider. Mulberries do seem to have been used for winemaking, although the result would probably have been nearer a melomel than a wine, as the fruit juice would no doubt have been diluted with water and sweetened with honey (sugar was virtually unobtainable and fabulously expensive). It seems that fruit wines did not become popular until the West Indies were colonized although, in 1635, a certain Francis Chamberlayne was granted an exclusive licence to make and sell wine from 'dried grapes or raysons'.

The beginning of the seventeenth century also saw the end of the long struggle over the use of hops in ale which had been heralded over two hundred years previously with that first imported beer. Brewing had become quite an industry and developed its own strong guild. Controls were enforced on the quality of the malt supplied, on the price of ale, on where and how it was brewed, on the measures in which it was supplied and even, by curfew, on the hours in which it could be sold. Controls were also enforced on coopers and the quality of their casks. The trade was quite well organized and regularly taxed and was in a good position to resist encroachment.

Once people had acquired a taste for the clean, tangy flavour of the new hopped beer, however, they began to prefer it to traditional ale. Soon, hops were imported from Holland and Belgium and some brewers began to brew beer. The struggle went on. The beer brewers organized themselves into a guild and petitioned for recognition, which was granted. Then the ale brewers petitioned that beer should be taxed, which was also granted. Some cities forbade the use of hops, but commercially they were on the losing side for hops not only flavoured ale but also helped to preserve it.

In 1624, a group of immigrant Huguenots

Monks of medieval Burgundy cultivating the vine.

settled in Kent in south-east England and planted the hops they had brought with them. The plants flourished and the hop-growing industry was soon established. All ales were flavoured and preserved with hops and the words ale and beer soon became synonymous. During the seventeenth and eighteenth centuries brewing moved from the home to commercial breweries in order to cater for the demand for better beer than that brewed by the tavern keeper.

The first Golden Age

In 1568, William Turner, a physician to Queen Elizabeth I, published the first book in England on the subject of wine. He recommended the drinking of white wines rather than red since he believed that red wines caused the accumulation of gravel in the gall bladder and kidneys. White wines, he thought, would cool and clean the system and prevent the formation of these stones which were very painful, no matter how small. In fact, the medicinal uses of wine in the medieval world were real: surgeon barbers used wine not only to cleanse wounds but also to stupefy their patients before the amputation of a limb, and country folk washed their cuts with wine or vinegar and brewed particular beverages as remedies for particular ailments. Herbs were often added to wine to relieve the pains of rheumatism or childbirth, and wine-based possets helped the elderly and the convalescent to take nourishment. (The success of these remedies can often be seen by the substantial ages recorded on the tombstones in country churchyards.)

In general new wine was preferred to old, but wine was sometimes kept for several years—resin would be added to prevent it from going sour. Wine was very cheap: Rhenish wine, malmsey, muscatel, claret, and sack (sherry) were the best known and most frequently drunk. Wine tended to be an after-dinner drink: breakfast and lunch would be washed down with ale. It was during the seventeenth and eighteenth centuries that native ingredients began to come into their own—the making of wine from fruits, flowers and vegetables; cider from apples; mead from honey; and cordials from fruits and brandy, reached their first Golden Age.

Towards the end of the seventeenth century several books were published on the subject of winemaking. Walter Charleton's *Mysterie of Vintners* recommended racking to clear cloudy wines:

The best time to rack wine is the decrease of the moon and when the wine is free from fretting; the wind being at the North East or North West and not at South, the sky serene, free from thunder and lightening.

In his *Vinetum Britannicum* of 1676, J Worlidge admits that 'wine made from the grape is the richest drink this world affords', but he points out that for the English climate perry, cider, cherry and gooseberry wines are better. He had found, however, that many English wines were too sweet and lacking in alcohol—a criticism which, unfortunately, still applies today in some cases.

In fact, much of the 'claret' or 'malmsey' sold to the general public contained large amounts of this English wine—the usual proportions were three parts English (made from fruits and flowers) to one part imported grape wine. Although the practice was dishonest and inflated prices were charged, many of these blends were very palatable drinks—blending has always been an important feature even of scrupulous winemaking.

With the invention of the cork in the eighteenth century by Dom Perignon (a very busy man indeed viticulturally—he also invented Champagne), the quality of wine improved. It no longer needed to be drunk young—in fact ageing became a positive asset, especially to the richer red wines.

More spirited drinks

Wine has been distilled in Europe since the Middle Ages, when alchemists, searching for the secret of immortality, produced a crude, harsh spirit which they called *aqua vitae*, the water of life. Apothecaries adopted it as the basic solution for their medicinal herbs and,

sweetened with honey, concoctions were served as cures for everything, including bubonic plague.

By the sixteenth century, monks in various monasteries from Ettal in Bavaria to Fécamp in Normandy were creating the forerunners of what we now call liqueurs. The best-known remain Benedictine, made by the monks at Fécamp, and Chartreuse, made by the Cistercian monks at Citeaux. Wild herbs were gathered from the local fields and woods, macerated in spirit and sweetened. The exact recipes, however, have always been a closely guarded secret.

As knowledge of these herbal liqueurs spread, fruit juices were mixed with the spirits. The still room became part of many households and was supervised by the lady of the house who produced spirits not only for drinking but

also for cosmetic and medicinal purposes. Today, of course, it is illegal to distill without a licence, although this is more a health safeguard than anything else since quite poisonous spirits can be produced by people with more enthusiasm than knowledge!

The New World

When the first French Huguenots arrived in North America between 1562 and 1564 they found wild Scuppernong grapes growing in Florida which they used to make wine. Wild grapes continued to be the main source of American wine until around the 1770's when the *vinifera* grape, the type grown in Europe, was introduced into California from Mexico. The Mission grape, a variety of *vinifera* had already been grown for winemaking at the Franciscan missions in New Mexico, to where it had originally been taken by Spanish explorers and missionaries. The next hundred years saw the growth of a flourishing wine industry in the area while in the East, where attempts to grow the *vinifera* grape had been unsuccessful, native varieties, beginning with the Alexander, were being domesticated.

With the opening of the first transcontinental railroad in 1869, wine from California became available in the East and a bitter East/West rivalry grew up among commercial winegrowers.

Then came the phylloxera epidemic which destroyed vast portions of vineyards in both Europe and California. The phylloxera was an American insect which lived mainly on the leaves of American vines and did them no great harm since natural selection had made their roots resistant. European vines, on the other hand, had no such immunity, but these were the varieties which produced better wine grapes. The phylloxera inflicted great damage on European vines grown in California but the growers there quickly discovered that grafting the vines on to native American stock saved them. In Europe the results were even more devastating and virtually the entire stock was destroyed. European viticulture was saved eventually by American roots grafted on to European vines. So every modern wine we drink is, technically, American in origin.

As winemaking slowly recovered from the phylloxera disaster, the first effects of the Prohibition movement started to be felt. One by one, states went 'dry' until 1919 when alcohol was outlawed completely throughout the United States. It seems likely however that the period of illegality—Prohibition was finally repealed in 1933—brought the home winemaker thoroughly into his own. Sacramental wine was still permitted by law and large amounts were sold through 'rabbis' as the use of wine in the home is required by the Jewish faith. Anyone could become a rabbi by presenting a list of his congregation (as often as not culled from the telephone book) and millions of people were recruited, without their knowledge, into fake synagogues!

Tonic wine, also still legal, was another favourite tipple as people quickly discovered that refrigeration caused the evil-tasting medical ingredients to sink to the bottom of the bottle, leaving a drinkable wine which could be decanted off. 'Wine bricks'—packages of pressed grapes—were widely marketed to growing numbers of home winemakers. A yeast pill was sold along with the grapes with strict instructions *not* to use it 'because if you do this will turn into wine which is illegal'.

The vine was also taken to South Africa and Australia by early immigrants and both countries were producing good wine by the middle of the nineteenth century. South Africa, in fact, was exporting the sweet, strong Constantia wine back to Europe by the end of the eighteenth century.

A similar story can be told for Australia. The early settlers were mostly rugged pioneers more accustomed to drinking beer than wine. As a result, and combined with a warm climate, brewing flourished so much that it became a major industry and was heavily taxed. Vines were first planted just north of Sydney (they arrived with the first fleet!) and slowly spread throughout the south-eastern part of the country. The founder of the Australian wine industry, by common consent, was a Scotsman called James Busby who planted vineyards in the Hunter Valley in New South Wales. Later,

German immigrants planted vines in the Barossa Valley, while other immigrants developed the Southern Vales, to the south of the city of Adelaide. Progress in commercial winemaking was interrupted by the phylloxera epidemic, which reached Australia via Europe and had an effect which was equally devastating—only Chateau Tahbilk in Victoria survived the epidemic. But after grafting, the resulting wines were better and stronger than anything produced before and the change in fashion from sweet dessert wines to dry table wines has enabled Australian producers to concentrate on producing good quality grape wines comparable with most European and Californian offerings.

From Pasteur to the present day

By 1814, domestic winemaking in Britain was a well established activity, judging from a book published by a certain Mr. Cushing. But his *Treatise on Family Wine Making* shows how little the process of fermentation was understood:

Medicine or staple diet?

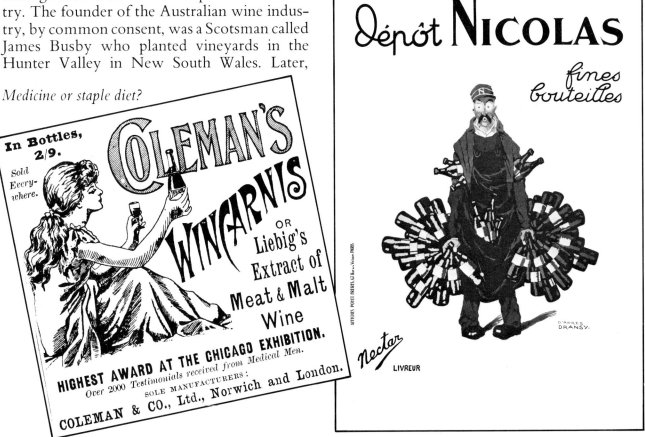

Vinous fermentation may be said to be a Divine operation which the Omniscient Creator has placed in our cup of life, to transmute the fruits of the Earth into Wine for the benefit and comfort of His creatures.

The activity of yeast, the unknown 'spirit' which caused fermentation has always been regarded as something of a mystery, even a miracle. Indeed, one of the popular old names for yeast was 'godisgood'.

Two years later in 1816, John MacCulloch produced a rather more scientific study of the subject, although he admitted that little was known about yeast. He strongly criticized some of the common practices of the day, such as the addition of brandy after fermentation and the use of too much sugar and raisins. One of MacCulloch's students, W. H. Roberts, went on to write a wonderfully practical book called *The British Wine-maker and Domestic Brewer* in 1835. Enthusiastically received by press and public alike, it recommended the use of an instrument called a 'saccharometer' to measure the quantity of sugar in a liquid. Now known as a hydrometer, it has become an essential piece of equipment for everyday winemaking.

It was with the discovery of the yeast cell by Pasteur in the 1860's that the process of fermentation was finally understood. But even as scientific understanding of winemaking and brewing grew, the industrial revolution and the consequent drift from the countryside to the towns began to take its toll on ancient customs. The Boer War, and more especially the First World War, saw the end of the great era of domestic winemaking and brewing. The herbs, fruits and flowers were not available in the towns; the back-to-back or terraced cottages were too small to permit activities of this kind; long hours and low wages were the final blow.

The making of country wines, ales and cordials virtually died out. But not quite. After the Second World War, servicemen and women returned from continental Europe where wine was the staff of life. The social revolution, begun by egalitarian rationing and aided by new technology, included a substantial reduction in the number of hours worked and a great improvement in the quality of life. Interest in both food and wine grew, and with it, interest in cooking and winemaking.

After 1945, a whole generation of eager new winemakers learned how to make wines from the few remaining country winemakers, and discovered the joys of making and drinking ales, meads and wines in the home. By the mid-1950's the tide had turned. The last thirty years has seen a resurgence of interest in 'country' activities all over the world. The interest includes the baking of bread, the growing of vegetables in organically fertilized soil, the brewing of sound strong beer and the making of finely flavoured wines in hygienic conditions. There is a rejection of the artificial, the 'ersatz', and a demand for naturally produced food and beverages. The following chapters will show you how to make a great range of country wines, ales, cordials, meads, vinegars, possets, punches, cups and beverages for every season, for all ages of man from childhood to old age. Drunk in moderation, they will undoubtedly promote health and maintain vigour—and provide hours of enjoyment both in the making and the drinking.

PUNCH, OR THE LONDON CHARIVARI.—April 26, 1911.

CALLING OUT THE RÉSERVE CUVÉE.

Gooseberry. "AHA! THIS OUGHT TO BE MY RECORD YEAR! SEE ME SPARKLE!"

Country Wines

In the course of time, almost every known plant has been used to flavour alcoholic drinks. Trial and error have therefore taught us which plants are dangerous or unsuitable and which make good wine – for instance, flowers give a delicate flavour and bouquet but lack body, acid and tannin; cereals and vegetables have enough body, but again lack tannin and acid; herbs and spices lend flavour but little else; leaves too, although they contain some tannin, need the addition of other ingredients to make a good wine. Fruit seems to contain more of the essential ingredients than any of the above and, of all the fruits, none has proved more successful than the grape. It comes closest to possessing just the right balance of acids, tannins, sugars, vitamins and minerals to produce an attractive taste and smell, and to help the yeast ferment the sugar into alcohol. Indeed, since yeast is naturally present on grape skins, the earliest wines were made simply by leaving vessels of crushed sweet grapes in a warm place to ferment spontaneously.

However, the grape is far from indispensable when it comes to making country wines, and the hedgerows and gardens of the countryside – not to mention the shops of the town – provide many substitutes that are far from inadequate. So what is needed to make a good wine? Let us look at each of the ingredients in turn before going on to consider how they can be transformed into the 'cup that cheers'.

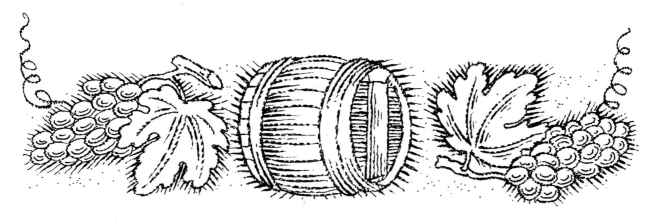

Ingredients

Flavouring Ingredients

Fruits Fruits tend to make better wines than other ingredients because they contain more acids and nitrogenous matter. Many early country wines were made simply by expressing the juice of a fruit or fruits and mixing that with a syrup of sugar boiled in water.

Traditionally, the quantity of fruit used per gallon of water was extremely high. Perhaps the fruit was of poorer quality than now, or perhaps palates then preferred a much stronger flavour; for whatever reason, wines were often extremely sweet and the use of less fruit would probably have produced a less tasty wine. A typical Victorian recipe for strawberry wine appeared in W. H. Roberts' definitive *The British Wine-maker and Domestic Brewer*:

'The same weight of water as juice is required for making this wine. The fruit, that it may be thoroughly bruised, should be squeezed in small portions, after being deprived of its stalks; the water is then added, well mixed with the fruit, and allowed to stand on it forty-eight hours; the mixture must then be pressed through a sieve into the fermenting tub, the juice and water measured, and the deficiency of quantity made up, by putting as much water upon the refuse of fruit as is necessary. The fruit must again be squeezed, and the juice strained into the former quantity. A portion should then be taken out for examination by the saccharometer, and the necessary weight of sugar put in.
'If the operator wishes the wine to be high in colour, 3 lbs. of beet-root should be washed, scraped, sliced, and put into the fermenting tub, and allowed to remain there until the casking. Two days before casking, 16 lbs. weight or more of strawberries must be tied up in a piece of thin muslin, and put in the fermenting tub, in order to impart to the wine a flavour of the fruit. As the process of fermentation in a great measure dissipates this flavour, the more fruit employed in this way the higher will be the aroma of the wine.

'Immediately before casking, the fruit is taken from the muslin and the juice, and squeezed through the sieve into the *must*. The fermentation will be complete without artificial means, provided it is carried on in a warm room. I have some of this wine twelve years old.'

Today, although some winemakers of repute still use as much as, say, 6 lb/2.7 kg of elder-berries to make only 1 Imperial gallon/4.5 litres (5 quarts) of wine, on the whole the trend is to use rather less fruit and to produce somewhat lighter and drier wines to be served as table wines rather than as the social and dessert wines produced by our forebears.

Methods of extracting the juice from the fruit have also changed. Until comparatively recently, it was usually extracted by steeping the fruit in water for up to three weeks at a time. Although the vessel would be covered with a

cloth of some kind, the floating fruit often developed a rich mould, as many traditional home winemakers could testify! Modern methods of juice extraction can prevent this problem, notably by the use of pectin-destroying enzymes protected by sulphite and shorter fermentation on the pulp.

Red juices from elderberries, blackberries, damsons and blackcurrants are best extracted by heating the crushed fruit to 176°F/85°C for 15 minutes or so, then cooling or pressing. This method produces wines with better colour, higher alcohol and less bitterness than when the fruit is fermented on the pulp—the traditional method for making red wine in Europe. Called 'heat treatment', this method is superior to boiling the fruit which tends to produce a 'cooked' flavour in the wine, and can be strongly recommended. Fruits that produce white wines can be treated in a similar way, although they should be heated to the lower temperature of 149°F/65°C. More often with white wine, however, the preference is to crush the fruit, add cold water, pectic enzyme and sulphite, cover and leave for twenty-four hours, and then ferment on the pulp for only

three to four days. This method extracts the desired soluble ingredients without too many of the bitter flavours that can develop from long fermentation on the pulp.

Steam juice extractors, once popular, are now thought to produce a 'cooked' flavour and hazes in the wine, and are consequently losing some of their appeal. Blending fruit is gaining in popularity. Some winemakers strain out the solids after blending and discard them, using only the juice which they then dilute to make the must. Others argue that many valuable ingredients remain in the solids and are therefore wasted if the fruit is not fermented on the pulp at all. Many now ferment white fruit wines on the pulp for a few days, and then strain out the solids.

An excellent rosé wine can be made, incidentally, from a 'second run' on the pressed pulp from an apple wine mixed with pulp from a black fruit wine, such as blackberry or elderberry, and with the addition of water, sugar and red or white grapes. This does tend to support the argument that much that is good is thrown away too soon!

All fruit should be cleaned and washed before it is crushed. Always use the best quality available since stale or damaged fruit may already be infected with spoilage organisms. If windfall or damaged fruit must be used, cut away all bruised parts and maggot holes and sterilize the rest in a double strength sulphite solution. Frozen fruit makes successful wine provided that it is sulphited before freezing—otherwise it tends to oxidize as it thaws.

Stones (pits) must always be removed from fruits, although some pips or seeds may be left in. Even more important, always avoid cracked stones. If any are included, the glycosides present in the kernels may be converted into a poison called hydrogen cyanide. Avoid, too, the white pith of citrus fruit. It contains not only an unacceptably bitter flavour, but also much pectin that causes haze in the wine.

Bananas are best used when the skins are black and the pulp brown. They are often used as an additive to wine and contribute body rather than flavour. One or two per Imperial gallon/4.5 litres (5 quarts) are enough. Pineapples must be trimmed but need not be peeled. Soft fruits must be cleaned from their stalks and washed in cold water.

Vegetables The method of extracting the juice from vegetables remains the same as it has always been. The vegetables are cleaned, scrubbed, diced and boiled in water until they are tender. The cooking liquor (into which most of the nutrients from the vegetables will be transferred as the water boils) is then used for making the wine; the cooked vegetables can either be eaten or thrown away.

Fresh and tender vegetables straight from the garden can be trimmed, scrubbed and blended without cooking, and the juice and pulp fermented on the pulp for just a few days. Do not leave them too long or the resulting flavour will be overpowering rather than subtle. Since vegetables must be blanched before they are frozen there is no point in using frozen vegetables to make wine. Indeed, the best vegetable wines are made from really fresh vegetables, and any stale or poor-quality produce should be avoided. The results are simply not worth the effort.

Vegetables contain little in the way of acid or tannin and it is wise therefore to add enough to make up the deficiency. The main contribution of vegetables to a wine is body and flavour.

Flowers The desire to capture the fragrance of flowers in wine reaches back for possibly several thousand years when they were first added to a fermenting honey must. Alas, flowers have even less to contribute to a wine than vegetables—nothing, in fact, but aroma and flavour. Everything else must be added, including body in the form of raisins or sultanas. Green leaves and stems should be avoided as they contribute a bitter flavour.

Flowers must be picked on a warm day when the blooms are fully open. Roses can be picked at petal fall but, where possible, other flowers should be picked as soon as they are fully open. Remove the petals or blooms from their stalks or calyx and place them in a large bowl. Pour on hot water and rub the petals gently with the back of a wooden spoon against the sides of the bowl. Cover and, when cool, add one Campden tablet and one teaspoonful/5 ml of citric acid. Macerate the blooms against the sides of the bowl twice a day for three days then strain out and press the petals to remove the liquid. Use only the liquor to make the must.

Leaves The most useful leaves are the summer prunings from vines and blackberry bushes; the young mature leaves of the blackcurrant bush; and the young mature leaves from the oak and walnut trees. Lime bracts are sometimes used, too, and of course tea leaves.

When the vine has fruited, excess foliage beyond the tiny bunch of grapes should be removed, leaving only one or two leaves to draw up the sap to feed the grapes rather than the extending shoots. Similarly, with blackberries—excessive side shoots must be kept in check. Cut the shoots with secateurs, wash them in clean running water, chop them up and pour boiling water over them. Apart from making a wine known as 'folly' (see page 97) from the French word *feuille* meaning leaf, these prunings may be added to other musts to improve vinosity and flavour. Blackcurrant, oak and walnut leaves should be treated in the same way. Only a small number are needed and are best used as an additive to other wines. They freeze successfully and can be used at your convenience.

Herbs Parsley is the herb most commonly made into wine, but many others were, and still can be, used—especially to make tonic or medicinal wines. Gather the herbs when they are at their best: roots when the plant is dormant; leaves when just fully grown and before the flowers appear; flowers when just fully out. Leaves and flowers should be gathered as soon as the dew has evaporated and before the sun has volatilized their essential oils. Handle them gently so as not to bruise them prematurely.

Herbs provide aroma and flavour only and everything else must be added to make wine. Prepare the essence from herb leaves and flowers in the same way as described for flowers. When the root is to be used, wash it clean, cut it up and boil until it is tender.

Spices The most popular spice for making wine is ginger root. However, it can only be used as a flavouring ingredient. Freshly dried root, well bruised to open up the centre, is best. Cloves, coriander and caraway seeds may also be used to flavour wine.

Saps Several trees are suitable for tapping to obtain sap for making into wine: the birch, the sycamore, the walnut, the date palm, the coconut palm and the sugar maple. Several varieties of birch are particularly suitable—the silver birch, common in eastern and southern England; the white birch, common in western and northern England; and the dwarf birch, which grows in Scotland. In the United States, the black birch or cherry birch is common from the northern states down to Florida. Because of its high sugar content, the sap is used for making birch beer, a distinctive-flavoured soft drink, and therefore should also produce a good wine.

Early spring is the best time for tapping trees since the sap is flowing abundantly just prior to the opening of the leaf buds. *Never* tap a young tree since you may easily kill it. A mature tree suitable for tapping will have a diameter of from 8-9 in/20-22.5 cm.

Cereals Cereals such as barley, maize (corn), millet, rice and wheat, can be used to make wines of a sort. Millet wine, for instance, is widely produced in the country areas of China while in Japan the national drink, *sake,* is a wine made from rice. Flaked versions of cereals should be used whenever possible. Cereals provide gluten or body to a wine and some nitrogenous material and flavour, but it is advisable also to add some sultanas or raisins and, of course, acid and tannin. A special yeast, called *Saccharomyces diastaticus,* should be used with cereal musts since it ferments out some of the starch. The goodness is extracted from cereals by pouring boiling water on the cracked or flaked grains and stirring well.

Other Essential Ingredients

Yeast In the earliest days of winemaking, fermentation was achieved by leaving a vessel of sweet grape juice in a warm place. The various yeasts and other fungi and bacteria naturally present on the grape skins decomposed the sugar, turning it into alcohol and carbon dioxide. Fermentation was regarded as a great mystery, a particularly appreciated act of God. When fruit wines were made, fermentation was, again, often left to the wild yeasts present on the fruit, unless the liquor was boiled—then ale or bread yeast was spread on a slice of toast which was floated on the surface of the must. (The bread provided the yeast cells with nourishment in the form of nitrogen and vitamin B.) The great dangers in using these methods were, of course, that the juice or must would be inadequately yeasted and that there would be a consequent risk of infection from unwanted spoilage yeast and bacteria.

Only during the past thirty years have special wine yeasts become available for use at home. They are marketed in several forms: as tablets; as putty-coloured granules; as liquids; and as a culture on an agar jelly slant in a sealed test tube.

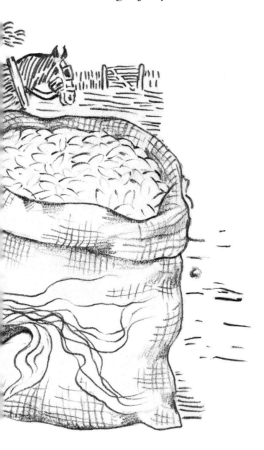

They are cultured in laboratories from pure yeast cells taken from grapes grown in areas that produce wines of distinctive styles, e.g. sherry, port, burgundy, claret, Sauternes, and so on.

These special yeasts are vastly superior to bakers' and brewers' yeasts, and should be used in winemaking whenever possible. They are also preferable to the wild yeasts and bacteria present on fruit. Apart from the beneficial yeast cells found on fruit, there are thousands of cells of spoilage fungi and bacteria mixed in with them and these pass into the wine. Often they cause 'off' flavours as well as preventing the wine yeast cells from fermenting adequately.

In place of the traditional slice of bread or toast which once floated on the must, modern winemakers now add the necessary nitrogen and vitamin B in the form of nutrient salts consisting of ammonium phosphate and ammonium sulphate, together with vitamin B. Grapes contain sufficient nutrient for the yeast and any recipes which contain a fair quota of grapes—whether fresh, dried as sultanas or raisins, or even liquid as concentrated grape juice—rarely need much, if any, additional nutrient. Granulated wine yeasts are often sold in sealed envelopes that also contain just enough nutrient to get the yeast cells off to a good start. Ingredients such as flowers, herbs and spices contain no nutrient and so one level teaspoonful/5 ml of ammonium phosphate or sulphate crystals per Imperial gallon/4.5 litres (5 quarts) should be added. The nutrient ensures a good fermentation and the conversion of the sugar to alcohol.

Clearly, a good wine yeast is an absolutely essential ingredient. To get the very best out of a good wine yeast it must be used in the proper way and under proper conditions—for instance, it ferments more efficiently if activated before it is added to the must, and also if all the wild yeasts and bacteria present in the must are killed or inhibited before it is added. To achieve a clean must, purify it with sulphite.

Sulphite The purifying qualities of sulphur have long been known to winemakers—sulphur candles used to be burned inside casks to kill off all spoilage organisms, originally called 'wild spirits'. Only in recent years has a compound of sulphur been developed that could be

some acid: some, such as blackcurrants and lemons, contain a great deal; others, such as dates and figs, contain very little, if any. Flowers, vegetables, herbs, grains and spices contain no acid worth mentioning. When fruits are diluted with water or when ingredients without acid are used, some acid must be added to ensure a good fermentation and a good flavour.

The three most common acids are *citric*, found in all citrus fruit; *malic* found in apples, among many other fruits; and *tartaric* found only in grapes, which also contain some malic and citric acids. There is some controversy among expert winemakers as to which acid to add to a wine, since each one has its advantages and disadvantages. The great majority have settled for citric acid, but some do still prefer to use a blend of all three. In making such a decision, consideration should be given both to the quantity and type of acid already present in the fruit—and obviously more will be needed in flower and vegetable wines than in fruit ones. You can add acid either by adding acid fruit such as lemons to the wine or by adding acid crystals. All of the individual recipes in this book take account of the need for acid and recommend suitable types and quantities. When adding citric acid, bear in mind that the juice of one lemon is roughly equivalent to one level teaspoonful/5 ml of crystals.

Tannin Tannin gives red wine character and bite, and the addition of a little tannin can improve the flavour of all wines; it also helps the keeping qualities. All grapes contain tannin in their stalks, skins and pips, while some other fruits, such as pears, elderberries and blackberries, contain it only in their skin. Other plants are woefully short. Tea contains tannin and some early post-World War II wine recipes recommend the addition of half a cupful of cold strong tea per gallon of liquid. Nowadays it is more usual (and perhaps more accurate!) to use grape tannin powder or liquid tannin at the rate of half to one level teaspoonful per Imperial gallon/2.5 to 5 ml per 4.5 litres (5 quarts).

Pectin-destroying enzyme Some fruits contain a lot of pectin, the substance which causes jams, marmalades and conserves to set. This quality is not, however, required in wine—indeed the very opposite is true! Pectin can also

safely added to liquids to purify them. Two compounds are now in common use in winemaking: potassium metabisulphite and sodium metabisulphite. Both are available commercially in white crystalline powder form or compressed and sold as Campden tablets. One Campden tablet is sufficient to clean one Imperial gallon/4.5 litres (5 quarts) of normal must, although two will be needed if the fruit is over-ripe or mouldy. Sulphite can, however, inhibit the activity of wine yeast and to avoid this possibility it is wise to add the sulphite to the must, then leave it for at least twenty-four hours before adding the yeast.

Acid Another essential ingredient is acid. Yeast thrives best in an acid solution, and acid is also necessary to give freshness to a wine; without a sufficient supply the finished wine will taste medicinal and will not keep. Most fruits contain

cause a wine to appear hazy unless it is removed. (Our forebears used to serve their wines in coloured glasses so that this haze would not be so noticeable.) We now know that pectin can be destroyed by enzymes that are usually present in fruits although not always in sufficient quantity to prevent a slight haze. It is sensible, then, to add a little pectin-destroying enzyme to those musts made from the fruits that are often used for jam-making: apricots, blackberries, blackcurrants, plums, raspberries and strawberries. When in doubt, a teaspoonful per Imperial gallon/5 ml per 4.5 litres (5 quarts) will always ensure the best possible juice extraction and a wine free from pectin haze.

Water Ingredients such as flowers, herbs, grains and spices contain no water, and vegetables contain very little. Fruits contain varying quantities of water in the form of juice up to three-quarters of their weight, but these fruit juices are often highly acidic and need to be diluted with water. Clean water is essential, then, in the making of country wines. In most countries, a clean safe water supply is available in every home, but fresh spring water is excellent, too, and well water is safe so long as no poisonous matter can drain into it. Rain water should always be filtered and boiled before use. It does not seem to matter significantly whether water is 'soft' or 'hard' although if there is a choice, preference should be given to a medium or slightly hard water, because the many trace elements that it contains may help to create a slightly better bouquet and flavour. Distilled water produces dull, characterless wines.

Some older country recipes recommend boiling water then leaving it until cold before using it—probably reflecting a fear of spoiling the wine by using impure water. The tradition does linger on, however, and some experts still recommend using cold boiled water, perhaps as one way of avoiding using water with chlorine, which is often added to reservoir water to purify it. Boiling drives off the chlorine, which can taint the wine and also precipitates a chalk, calcium carbonate, which might reduce the acidity of the must. In most places and in most cases, however, ordinary tap water is perfectly adequate and safe to use. But if you are ever in doubt, boil the water first and then cool it—'It's better to be safe than sorry.'

Sugar Apart from grapes grown in a warm atmosphere, no ingredient used for making wine contains enough natural sugar to ensure the creation of sufficient alcohol to make a good wine. Even grapes grown in Burgundy and throughout Germany sometimes do not develop sufficient natural sugar to make an adequate wine. Sugar is therefore added when necessary to help nature along.

Traditional recipes frequently called for the addition of 4 lb of sugar per Imperial gallon of liquid/2 kg per 4.5 litres (8 cups per 5 quarts), but sugar in those days was less pure than it is today and contained a quantity of unfermentable matter; in addition, the common preference was for very much sweeter wines than is the norm today. An instrument called a saccharometer, which measured the approximate quantity of sugar in a must, was used more than 200 years ago. Today this same simple instrument is still used but is now called a hydrometer. (Its use is described on page 34.) With its aid, the winemaker can control the quantity of additional sugar that must be added to produce a wine of approximately a given alcohol content.

The type of sugar added is of some importance. The least expensive and the most suitable is ordinary white granulated sugar. It is 99.95 per cent pure and there is no chemical difference between beet and cane varieties. Light brown and dark brown sugars can also be used but they do impart both colour and flavour to wine and, clearly, are not to be recommended for white and golden wines unless, of course, you wish to create a tawny wine with a caramel overtone.

Before the advent of sugar, honey was used as a sweetener but it produced a mead rather than a wine for the honey taste dominated other flavours. A little white honey could be used effectively in flower wines but not more than 1 lb per Imperial gallon/450 g per 4.5 litres (5 quarts). The quantity of granulated sugar should be reduced by ¾ lb/350 g (1½ cups) if honey is used.

There is no point in using cube, lump or loaf sugar since they are the same as granulated but more expensive because of their shaping process. Caster (superfine) sugar dissolves very quickly, as does icing (confectioners') sugar, but both are more expensive in the shops than the granulated variety – although they are all chemically the same.

Milk sugar, called lactose, cannot be fermented by wine yeasts but is sometimes used to sweeten wines. It has only one-third of the sweetening power of granulated sugar, so you may have to use quite a lot of it to obtain the sweetness you desire. Used at the rate of 3-4 oz per Imperial gallon/75-100 g per 4.5 litres (⅓ cup per 5 quarts), however, it can take the edge off a very dry wine.

Golden (light corn) syrup may be used in much the same way as honey, with a similar rate of reduction in the amount of granulated sugar used. Like honey, about 25 per cent of the weight of syrup is water, so 1 lb/450 g of honey or golden (light corn) syrup is the equivalent of ¾ lb/350 g (1½ cups) of sugar.

Black treacle and molasses contain little fermentable sugar and possess an overpowering and unacceptable flavour. Not more than one tablespoonful per Imperial gallon/15 ml per 4.5 litres (5 quarts) should be used for colouring or medicinal purposes if so required.

Invert sugar is simply ordinary granulated sugar that has been split into its two component sugars—fructose and glucose. Yeast cells can ferment fructose and glucose immediately but ordinary sugar must first be split into the two by the enzyme called invertase which is secreted by the yeast cells. Ordinary sugar can be easily split into invert sugar: just boil 2 lb/900 g of granulated sugar in 1 Imperial pint/550 ml (2½ cups) of water containing one level teaspoonful/5 ml of citric acid crystals for about 20 minutes—when cool you have 2 Imperial pints/1.2 litres (5 cups) of invert sugar with a specific gravity of 1.300. Fructose and glucose powder are also available and can be used, although they are both more expensive than granulated sugar.

Finings A variety of ingredients can be used to remove the haze that sometimes remains in a wine, even after the use of a pectin-destroying enzyme. Our forebears used ox blood, milk or white of egg and all of these are still effective. Isinglass, marketed in the form of a gel, is now more popular, however. Bentonite, also marketed as a gel, is often used, so, too, is gelatine. These also remove some tannin which must be replaced. Directions for use are always given on the container.

These then are the ingredients necessary to the making of country wines of quality. They take account not only of the primary flavour of the finished article but also take advantage of modern advances in hygiene and fermentation, and control of acids and tannins. They allow us to produce wines which not only taste authentic and delicious but are the equal of many store-bought wines.

Ingredients to Avoid

One of the great joys of making country wines is the opportunity to experiment with different fruits, flowers, vegetables, herbs, spices and cereals, and with varying combinations of them. This is great fun and sometimes produces some very attractive and unusual wines. You must be careful not to allow your enthusiasm to run too wild, however, for some plants are poisonous and should not be used. This does not mean that wine made from these berries, flowers, leaves or roots will kill you; but they may taste nasty and in general make you feel unwell.

A list of known dangerous plants is given below but it is not exhaustive. *As a wise rule of thumb, do not use anything that you could not safely give a child to eat.*

Acacia, aconite, alder, anemone, aquilegia, azalea;

28

Baneberry, belladonna, berberis, bitter almond, bay tree leaves, beech nuts, box tree leaves, black nightshade, bindweed, bluebell, bryony, broom, buckthorn, buddleia, buttercup;

Campion, celandine, charlock, cineraria, clematis, clover, cotoneaster, columbine, cow-bane, crocus, crowfoot, chrysanthemum, cuckoo-pint, cyclamen;

Daffodil, dahlia, deadly nightshade, delphinium, dwarf elder;

Fool's parsley, figwort, foxglove, fungi of all kinds;

Geranium, gladiolus, goosefoot, green potatoes;

All members of the helebore family, hemlock, henbane, holly, honeysuckle (both flowers and berries), horse chestnut flowers and conkers, hydrangea, hyacinth;

Iris, ivy;

Jasmine, jonquil;

Laburnum, laurel, lilac, lilies of the valley, lilies of all kinds, lobelia, lucerne, lupins;

Marsh marigolds, meadow rue, mezereon, mistletoe, monkshood;

Narcissus;

Orchids;

Pheasant's eye, peony, poppy, privet;

Ragwort, rhododendron, rhubarb leaves;

Snowdrop, spearwort, spindleberries, spurge, sweet pea;

Thorn apple, tobacco plant, tomato stems and leaves, traveller's joy, tulip;

Wood anemone, woody nightshade;

Yew.

Equipment

Certain items of equipment are necessary to practise the craft of winemaking. In actual fact, the expense involved in acquiring the basic essentials is surprisingly modest and most investment in 'luxury' equipment can be left until such time as you feel sufficiently enthusiastic about your hobby to indulge in the extra expense. Many common items of household kitchen equipment can also be pressed into service, reducing even further the basic outlay necessary before you can start to make your own wine.

First, though, some general rules:

1.) Always avoid the following: lead-glazed earthenware jars; lead piping; zinc baths, buckets or boilers; chipped enamel pails, funnels, saucepans or containers; brass or copper pans or other utensils. Acids in wine react with the exposed metals mentioned above to form poisonous salts.

2.) Never use metal utensils unless they are made of silver or the best quality stainless steel. High grade aluminium pans may be used briefly for boiling low acid ingredients, but the contents of the pan should never be allowed to stand in the vessel for any length of time.

3.) Coloured polythene (plastic) equipment is also suspect. Cadmium, which is poisonous, is sometimes used for colouring, and the plasticizer can react with the acid or alcohol. It is always safer to use the natural plastic, polypropylene or polycarbonate utensils sold in home brew shops or department stores.

Main Essentials

Mashing bin The first item of equipment you will need is a vessel in which to mash fruit (or vegetables if you use the pulping method for very fresh produce) and prepare the must for conversion into wine. There was a time when glazed earthenware crocks and oak tubs, cut in half, were used, but when polythene (plastic) first became available in the 1950's, small trash bins with lids of this material became popular. Nowadays, however, purpose-made polythene (plastic) bins have largely taken their place.

These bins are natural and colourless, inert to acids and are light and easy to clean. They come supplied with close-fitting lids. They are sufficiently translucent for you to be able to see the level of the liquid inside and most of them are graduated both in metric and imperial measurements of volume, and in American standard sizes in the U.S. Standard sizes can contain 12, 15 or 25 litres of liquid, sufficient to make 2, 3 or 5 gallons of wine, respectively. It is unwise to fill them too full, even although each bin is fitted with a strong carrying handle, for they are flexible and the contents could spill when carried. The number of bins you require depends on the quantity of wine you intend to make at any one time, but certainly several, of different size, would be useful. They are easy to store, too, especially if you buy graded sizes, for they can stack inside one another when not in use.

Masher You will also need something with which to crush the fruit or vegetables. A potato masher is excellent for soft fruits, provided that it is made from nylon, stainless steel or heavily coated chrome. Other metals should be avoided.

A block of oak or other heavy non-resinous wood on the end of a broom handle does well for crushing harder fruits and vegetables. Purpose-made mangle-like fruit crushers can be bought if larger quantities have to be handled regularly, but they are too bulky and expensive if you propose to make only a few gallons of wine at a time. Electric blenders are becoming increasingly popular 'mashers', and steam juice extractors can also be used. Mincing and meat grinding machines may be used subject to the proviso that has already been mentioned about metal.

A recent innovation is a stainless steel blade on a shaft of the same metal that can be fitted to an electric drill. To use it, fit the lid of a bin between the blade and the drill and fill the bin with washed and perfect fruit. Now fit the lid to the bin, switch on, move the spinning blade up and down a few times and the fruit will be splendidly pulped.

Fermentation vessel Fermentation can be carried out in a mashing bin—indeed, this is essential when fermenting on the pulp. Some mashing bin lids are fitted with a grommet that can be removed so that an airlock can be fitted. This is especially useful when fermenting more than an Imperial gallon/4.5 litres (5 quarts) of must. More sophisticated bins are fitted with a draw-off tap at the bottom.

The vast majority of winemakers today, however, use colourless glass demijohns called jars or jugs for fermenting their wines. In the UK they are currently available in half and one gallon sizes/2.3 and 4.5 litres, but many hold slightly more—some up to as much as 5 litres. They are, nevertheless, widely referred to as 'gallon jars'. They are ideal for the purpose because they are inert to acids; can be easily washed and sterilized; activity in them can be seen; the narrow neck takes a bored bung and airlock that seals the jar effectively; and most have small carrying handles fitted to the neck. Their disadvantage is that they are brittle and are, therefore, breakable if not handled with care. They have also become quite expensive. They are so convenient, however, that they are frequently used for storage as well as fermentation. Since it may be necessary to store for a year before bottling, possession of several jars at least is essential for the active winemaker. Some larger glass carboys in a protective cover are also available in 25 and 55 litre sizes (which can make 5½ and 12¼ gallons of must, respectively).

An unbreakable transparent polycarbonate container has now been developed but is still at present rather expensive for popular use. A laminated polythene (plastic) bag containing a nylon 66 or Sarinex centre layer that makes it vapour-proof has also recently been marketed. It is fitted with a rigid neck to accommodate a bored bung and airlock, and a tap-like cover, and is supported in a vinyl-coated cardboard carton. It is now widely available in the United States and in Australia where wine is sold in bags and boxes of this type. It is unbreakable, easy to clean and sterilize, and can be used for fermentation, storage and serving. It can also be folded away when not in use.

Storage vessels Glass fermentation vessels can also be used for storage. If you have a limited supply of demijohns but access to glazed earthenware jars then these can be used instead. Although they are heavy to handle and vulnerable if used carelessly, they do have the advantage of insulating the wine from sudden changes in temperature, and they keep it cool and dark. Oak casks may, of course, also be used and these are especially recommended to mature red wines in quantities of 5½ gallons/25 litres (27½ quarts) and more. Smaller casks are not suitable because the ratio of surface to volume causes excessive oxidation of the wine.

Polythene (plastic) containers are not suitable since they are not vapour-proof. Plastic casks of the type used for draught beer can sometimes be used for the temporary storage of wine but there is still some slight uncertainty about the solubility of plastic in the presence of alcohol over a long period of time.

Airlocks Airlocks, or water seals as they are sometimes called, are used to exclude air from the must during fermentation while permitting gas to escape. There are several types that come in many different shapes and sizes but all work on the same principle. There are two main types. One is U-shaped with a spherical bulb on each wing of the 'U', and usually made of glass, the other consists of a small cylinder into which is fitted a narrower cylinder, and is usually made of plastic. Both end in a short tube which fits into a bored bung. A little water or sulphite solution is poured into the container thus forming a lock. It is then fitted into the hole in the bung, which is pushed into the neck of the fermentation jar in order to form an airtight seal. The gas given off during fermentation will

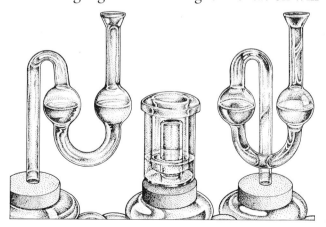

Various examples of the airlock. Whatever design is used, the bung should form an airtight seal.

build up sufficient pressure to force its way through the water or sulphite solution and escape into the outside air with a quiet 'plop'. The progress of fermentation can thus be very easily monitored.

Siphon A siphon, at its simplest, is a long length of rubber or plastic tubing which is used at the end of the fermentation period to suck off the new wine from its sediment. More sophisticated versions can be fitted with a glass J-tube at one end and a small tap at the other, or with a blocked end above which four holes have been drilled. To use the siphon, one end of the tube is inserted into the wine which must then be sucked into the tube until it is full. The outer end is temporarily closed and placed into a sterilized container for storage situated at a

lower level than the wine vessel. The tube is then opened and the wine will flow steadily into the lower vessel. This should be done carefully since it is imperative not to disturb the sediment and suck that up too, which would destroy the object of the exercise. The J-tube siphon sucks the wine down from the top and the blocked end type sucks it in from the sides; both therefore leave the sediment undisturbed and so are to be preferred to the simple tube. Also available is a larger siphon which is fitted with a small hand pump in the centre to save sucking the wine through by mouth.

Hydrometer Almost the only scientific, although simple, instrument required in amateur winemaking is the hydrometer (sometimes called a saccharometer) which, in appear-

ance, resembles a thermometer. The stem contains a graduation of figures which indicate the gravity or weight of the volume of liquid being measured compared with the same volume of water. In home winemaking and brewing the additional weight is almost entirely sugar so the instrument for all practical purposes measures the quantity of sugar dissolved in a must, and thus enables you to calculate how much additional sugar to add to produce a wine of a given alcoholic content. It is used in conjunction with a slim jar slightly taller than the hydrometer, which is called 'trial jar'. Some liquid to be tested is poured into the trial jar and the hydrometer inserted into it to measure the quantity of sugar present.

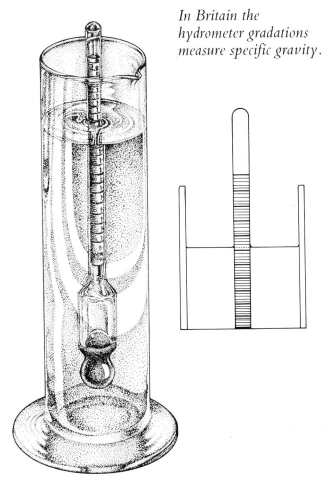

In Britain the hydrometer gradations measure specific gravity.

Hydrometers have different gradations in different countries. In the United States, the Brix or Balling gradation measures the percentage sugar content of the liquid being tested. In Australia the Beaumé gradation indicates the potential alcohol content of the must if it is fermented to dryness. A chart showing the relation between the different gradations is given on page 180.

Bottles You will need wine bottles, preferably of coloured glass to exclude the light, in which to age your wine. Use empty commercial wine bottles, after first soaking off old labels. Wash, drain, dry and store them upside down in a bottle carton until required. A bottle brush would be useful to clean congealed sediment from the sides and the bottle punt. Larger brushes might be required to clean demijohns, particularly under the shoulder which often becomes marked from matter thrown up during fermentation.

Corks and labels Cylindrical corks and a corking tool to insert them in the bottles are essential. The corking tool can be a simple flogger, a shaped cylinder in which the softened cork is placed and then hammered via a wooden piston into the bottle, or a hand machine in which the cork is levered into the bottle. Decorative labels and coloured foil or plastic capsules complete the professional appearance of the bottle.

Wine racks You will need somewhere to store the finished bottles of wine, and a wine rack is both a desirable acquisition and a sensible one for this purpose. Traditional wooden and metal racks can be purchased to fit any storage space and any number of bottles. Other metal, wooden or plastic bottle crates can be used, of course, including strong cardboard bottle cartons. But these do vary in quality and strength and only the strongest are safe when stored on their sides.

Record cards You should complete a record card for each wine you make, giving details of ingredients, quantities, methods, dates and results. The cards can be purchased ready printed or devised from a luggage label.

Smaller items Many homes will already have a number of the smaller pieces of equipment useful to a winemaker—items such as wooden spoons, measuring jugs, a pair of kitchen scales, a polythene (plastic) funnel or two, a nylon strainer, perhaps a kitchen thermometer and a preserving or large boiling pan. Such items need not be exclusively reserved for winemaking, although care should be taken to wash and sterilize them before use. It is best to avoid using utensils or equipment used in the making of pickles and chutneys.

Filters are occasionally used by winemakers. A supply of filter pads or pulp will be required each time the filter is used.

Useful Extras

Heaters Fermentation needs to be conducted in a place of at least moderate warmth. In very cold places it may be necessary to stand the jar on a thermal pad or surround it with a thermal belt to provide the necessary warmth. Suitable immersion heaters are also available and their advantage is that they can be attached to a thermostat to maintain the right temperature throughout the fermentation. Some winemakers adapt cupboards with insulation and electric 'black-heat' cylinders. In very warm weather it may, conversely, be necessary to provide some means of cooling the jars of must with fans or cold water.

Fruit press If you intend to make a great deal of fruit wine, you might wish to consider purchasing a fruit press—in fact, if you intend to make cider regularly, then you will require one. It is basically a wooden box with an open top and slotted sides through which the extracted juice flows into its base. Special pulp bags are usually available with a fruit press. To use the press wash it with a sulphite solution, then place the bag of pulp in the press. Pressure should be erratic rather than steady. As the flow begins to slow down, increase the pressure then leave it until the flow slows again, then increase the pressure again and so on. After a while, release the pressure entirely, remove the bag, stir up the pulp, replace the bag in the press and resume the pressure. Continue these processes until the pulp becomes a dry 'cake'.

Hygiene

All equipment must be kept clean, and sterilized before use. A chlorine-based sterilizer is excellent for removing stains and cleaning dirty jars and bottles as well as plastic vessels. Equipment so sterilized should be thoroughly rinsed in cold water to remove the chlorine. Chlorine-based sterilizers should never be used to sterilize ingredients, only equipment.

Sodium metabisulphite, especially when reinforced with citric acid, makes an effective sterilizing agent, especially for equipment that is otherwise clean. It is also safe and strongly recommended for sterilizing ingredients, especially fruit. This agent has the additional advantage of being an anti-oxidant, in other words it prevents oxidation or browning and the consequent deterioration in colour, bouquet and flavour.

Sodium metabisulphite is available as a powder and in tablet form, sold under the name Campden. One Campden tablet contains 0.44 g of sodium metabisulphite and releases 50 parts per million of the sterilizing bactericide and fungicide, sulphur dioxide, when dissolved in one Imperial gallon/4.5 litres (5 quarts) of water, must, wine, mead or cider. This is a normal and adequate dose but may safely be doubled or trebled when necessary.

Some winemakers dissolve the powder and some citric acid in water and keep this solution well sealed in a suitable bottle stored in a cool place. In these circumstances, it will retain its sterilizing power for several months.

To make up a typical solution, dissolve 100 g of sodium metabisulphite and 10 g of citric acid in 1 litre of cold water or 2 oz (¼ cup) of sodium metabisulphite and 1 level teaspoonful citric acid in 1 pint (2½ cups) of cold water. One teaspoonful/5 ml of either of the above solutions is equal to one Campden tablet.

One Campden tablet or one teaspoonful/5 ml of the solution dissolved in 1 Imperial pint/550 ml of cold water makes a powerful sterilizing solution for finally rinsing jars, bottles, corks and all other equipment before use. One tablet or one teaspoonful/5 ml in half an Imperial gallon of water/2.25 litres (2½ quarts) is adequate for washing fruit before use. One Campden tablet or one teaspoonful/5 ml added to one Imperial gallon/4.5 litres (5 quarts) of wine after racking prevents infection and oxidation. The wise use of sulphite prevents countless ailments and ensures sound wine.

Sodium metabisulphite and potassium metabisulphite are quite cheap. Campden tablets are a little more expensive but no winemaker should ever be without an adequate stock.

Making Wines

Since the end of the 1950's there has been a revolution in the craft of winemaking, both commercially and domestically. The classic wines of commerce may not have become much greater, but there is no doubt that everyday wines have improved enormously.

The new technology really started a century earlier with Pasteur's experiments. He not only proved that yeast caused fermentation, but also showed that there were many spoilage organisms present in musts that could be killed off by heat. Since then, more knowledge and understanding of how yeast works, better yeast strains, and above all, better hygiene, have all contributed to improving and controlling the craft of commercial and country winemaking.

Hygiene, for instance, was rudimentary in the early days: Campden tablets were known for their preservative qualities before 1940 but it is only since the early 1960's that their efficiency as a sterilizer of both equipment and ingredients has become widely known. Nowadays, no sensible winemaker fails to rinse equipment of all kinds immediately before use with a solution of sodium metabisulphite and citric acid, for we know that failure to do so could produce a wine that is tainted and spoiled. The risk is simply not worthwhile. **In fact, the regular use of Campden tablets is now so much a part of the routine of the craft of winemaking, that specific quantities are not mentioned in the list of ingredients in the recipes which follow.** It is taken for granted that every winemaker will always have them in stock and use them as and when required.

Similarly, the purity of yeast now available and the habit of adding a cultured wine yeast to a sterilized must has also improved the quality of country wines enormously. Some old recipes omitted yeast and left the must to chance, assuming that a miracle would happen and turn the must into wine; others included bakers' or brewers' yeast spread on a slice of toast. No sensible winemaker would do these things today. A pure yeast culture must always be used, preferably one activated before adding it to the must.

The use of better equipment has also improved the quality of wines. Natural polythene (plastic) bins are far easier to handle, clean and sterilize than old oak casks. And instead of laying a tile over the bung hole of the cask, we now know that airlocks not only keep out spoilage organisms invisibly floating in the air, but also encourage the yeast to obtain the energy it requires for living from the sugar in the must. This stimulates the fermentation and enables us to produce dry table wines in which all the sugar has been converted into alcohol and carbon dioxide.

Finally, the wider use today of the hydrometer enables us to control the amount of sugar we use and therefore the alcoholic strength of our wines. Country wines are no longer the oversweet cordials containing little alcohol that once they were. Nowadays, even an absolute beginner can choose the alcoholic content of his wine and therefore to some extent its sweetness or dryness. As a guide, all of the recipes in this book recommend a specific quantity of sugar appropriate to the wine and the ingredients, but this can never be more than approximate. The precise quantity will depend entirely on the natural sweetness of the other ingredients used and how much alcohol you want in your wine and this you, with the help of your hydrometer, can now determine as you go along.

That, then, is the background. Now the three modern processes of preparation, fermentation and maturation can be discussed in detail.

Preparation

First, the various primary ingredients must be assembled and prepared: select your fruit, vegetables, flowers, herbs, leaves, saps, cereal or spice, clean as necessary and place in a bin for pulp fermentation or into a jar if it is all liquid. If you are making a fruit wine, add pectic enzyme and one Campden tablet per Imperial gallon/4.5 litres (5 quarts) at this point to dissolve the pectin. Leave for twenty-four hours.

Using your hydrometer Next day, take your

first hydrometer reading to discover the sugar content of the must. Strain a quantity of the must into a trial jar and place the hydrometer in the jar. Wait until it stops bobbing and twisting. When it is quite still it will float and the surface of the must will indicate a reading on the chart of the stem. (In an apple must, for example, the reading might be 1.032, in a grape must it might be as high as 1.076. A flower or herb must without sultanas or seedless raisins or sugar could read only 1.002 and a vegetable must 1.006.)

Refer to the table on page 180. Find your hydrometer reading in the left-hand column. Level with it in column 3 you will find the weight of the sugar already present in your gallon of must. Make a note of this figure. Now look at the potential alcohol table in the right-hand column and select the approximate amount of alcohol you would like in your finished wine. Looking again at column 3, you will find level with the alcohol percentage, the *total* amount of sugar that you will need in your must. From this deduct the amount of sugar already present. The difference is the amount of sugar to add. If sultanas or raisins are to be included in the recipe, you will need to allow for their natural sugar content. Approximately two-thirds of their weight consists of fermentable sugars.

An example: The hydrometer reading of your fruit must is 1.020. This is equal to 9 oz/275 g (1 heaped cup) of sugar in the gallon. You are planning to add ½ lb/225 g (1 cup) of sultanas or raisins, the equivalent of 5 oz/150 g (⅔ cup) of sugar in the gallon/4.5 litres (5 quarts). So already accounted for is the equivalent of 14 oz/400 g (1¾ cups) of sugar. You would like an alcohol content of 12 per cent in the finished wine and the table indicates that a total of 2 lb 6½ oz/1100 g (scant 5 cups) of sugar will be needed. Deduct the 14 oz/400 g (1¾ cups) already accounted for, and you will see that 1 lb 8½ oz/700 g (heaped 3 cups) of sugar still needs to be added. Of course, merely by adding sugar, you will increase the volume of the must. To allow for that increase, you will need to add one-eighth more sugar than indicated in the table, in this case, about another 3 oz/90 g (⅓ cup). So the total amount of additional sugar will be 1 lb 11 oz/800 g (3½ cups).

But many country wines, especially those made from a vegetable, cereal or herb base are often stronger than 12 per cent. Moreover, some winemakers prefer to drink their wines not with meals but on social occasions. A larger quantity of sugar is therefore necessary, not only to increase the alcohol content slightly but also to sweeten the wine to some extent. The recipes in this book have taken into account not only the average sugar content of the base ingredient and the sugar content of the sultanas or raisins, but also the probable alcohol content and the increased volume of must in recommending the approximate amount of sugar to add. Nevertheless, it is a proper practice to take hydrometer readings and to adjust the added sugar accordingly.

Acid and tannin The acid and tannin content of the wine need to be considered now. Many recipes recommend the inclusion of acid in the form of lemon and/or orange juice because this was the traditional form of adding acid. The zest in citrus fruit skin can also add emphasis to the flavour of the base ingredient. But these

fruits may be replaced with citric acid crystals if this is more convenient. Generally, a non-acid base needs two level teaspoonfuls/10 ml for a light dry wine and three to four/15 to 20 ml for a sweeter, stronger wine. Fruit wines need less, depending on the acidity of the fruit. For example, blackcurrants need no extra acid at all, while dates and figs contain no acid and need a full quantity.

Tannin improves the character and longevity of a wine, especially fruit wines. Black grapes, elderberries, blackberries and pears usually contain sufficient tannin in their skins, but other fruits, especially those used to make a red wine, need the addition of up to one teaspoonful/5 ml of tannin powder or half a cup of cold tea.

Start your records. Assemble and prepare the equipment and ingredients.

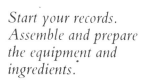

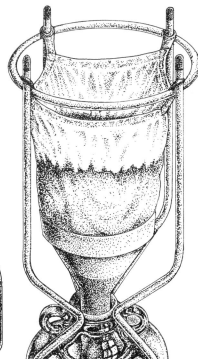

Strain the must into a jar, and press until dry.

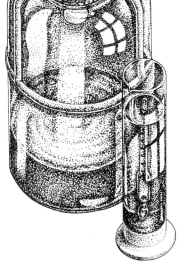

Fit an airlock and continue fermentation.

The basic must is now prepared with the right amount of sugar, acid and tannin; the next stage is to add the yeast so that fermentation may begin.

Fermentation

It is important to use a pure wine yeast, prefer- ably already activated, to ferment wine. Follow the instructions supplied with the tablet, sachet or phial of yeast to activate it. Alternatively, you can dissolve the juice of half an orange with a teaspoonful/5 ml of sugar and the wine yeast in a cupful of cold boiled water. Leave the mixture loosely covered in a warm place for a few hours—you will soon see signs of activity.

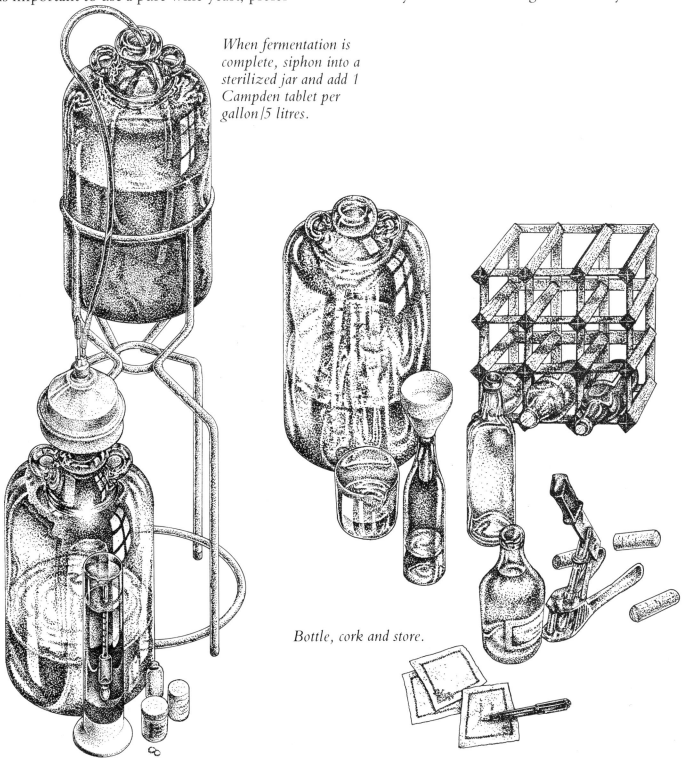

When fermentation is complete, siphon into a sterilized jar and add 1 Campden tablet per gallon/5 litres.

Bottle, cork and store.

Yeast cells also need some nourishment in the form of nitrogen, which they can obtain from most fruits and vegetables or from ammonium salts. A small quantity of nutrient salts is usually enclosed in the sachet with the yeast, but if you are using a liquid or tablet yeast then add half a teaspoonful/2.5 ml of nutrient salts to the must—especially when the base is flowers, leaves or herbs, even if a small quantity of raisins or sultanas is also being used.

Yeast ferments best between 59°F/15°C and 75°F/24°C, but will tolerate both lower and higher temperatures. It prefers a steady, even, unfluctuating temperature but, again, is tolerant of minor fluctuations. Experience shows that white wines develop best when fermented at around 61°F/16°C and red wines when fermented at around 68°F/20°C.

Fermenting on the pulp Fermentation on the pulp is usually conducted in a polythene (plastic) bin in which there is a certain amount of headroom. Keep the bin loosely covered with a clean towel or similar thick cloth, or with a sheet of polythene (plastic) tied down with wool, string or thin elastic, so that the dust and microbes can be kept out yet the fermentation gas can escape. The pulp should be kept submerged with a sterilized dinner plate or with something similar—but with nothing metallic. If this is not possible, press the pulp down into the must twice each day. This is important for, clearly, the goodness cannot be extracted from ingredients that are floating above the must. And there is also always the danger that the pulp might become the breeding ground for spoilage organisms, especially *Mycoderma aceti*, the vinegar bacillus.

Fermentation on the pulp should not extend beyond a few days since unwanted substances tend to get extracted by the increasing quantity of alcohol as it is being formed.

Straining After the first fermentation on the pulp, strain out the pulp through a nylon strainer or bag and drain dry. If the material is still fairly hard it should be pressed to extract as much juice as possible. You can use your hands or a small fruit press for this (see page 35). When the pulp is dry, remove it from the bag.

Fermenting out Stir the relevant amount of sugar into the strained must. Sometimes frothing will occur; always stir the sugar until it has dissolved. When the frothing has subsided, pour the must into a fermentation jar. Fit an airlock into the jar. Soften the bored bung in warm water and then screw the stem of the airlock into the hole in the bung until it fits tightly. In the same way, screw the bung into the neck of the jar until it will go no further. Finally, pour in a little sulphite solution to form the lock, tie on a completed record card or label and leave the jar in a warm position.

If you are using a standard demijohn and are making an Imperial gallon/4.5 litres (5 quarts) of wine, then the water, sugar and possibly juice from the base ingredient will produce more than enough must to fill the jar. Pour the excess into a sterilized bottle placed alongside the jar. The neck of the bottle should be plugged with cotton wool to keep out dust and micro-organisms, yet still allow the carbon dioxide to escape.

Normally fermentation takes about three weeks. Sometimes, however, with a strong

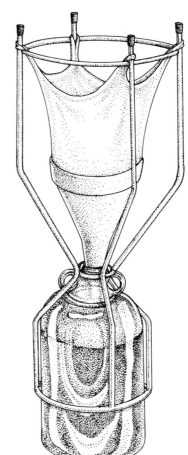

When the initial fermentation is complete, the must is strained and pressed dry.

40

yeast, the right temperature and the perfect balance of acid and nutrient, fermentation will finish in a week. On other occasions it may take six weeks or even longer, especially in low temperatures. There is nothing wrong, and long, slow fermentations are thought to produce the best flavoured wines. On rare occasions, fermentation will stop before it is expected to do so. First check with the hydrometer that the specific gravity of the must remains high. If fermentation has finished because all the sugar has been converted into alcohol and carbon dioxide, the hydrometer will sink in the new wine until the reading shows between 0.990 and 1.000. If this is so, the next stage of maturation can begin.

A 'stuck' fermentation If the reading is still quite high, however, say 1.042, then fermentation has become 'stuck' for some reason. It may be that the must has become too hot or too cold and the yeast is, therefore, inhibited. Move the jar to a different place where the temperature is appropriate and steady. Meanwhile, check over the record card and make sure that you have included sufficient acid and nutrient as recommended in the recipe, for a lack of either could cause fermentation to stick. If in any doubt, remedy the situation at once, by adding the quantity of acid recommended in the recipe and about half a teaspoonful/2.5 ml of yeast nutrient.

If fermentation does not soon start as a result of your actions, pour the contents of the jar into another jar, splashing the must into the receiving jar so that a quantity of oxygen is absorbed and the yeast stimulated to enlarge its colony.

The record card may also indicate that so much sugar was added that the yeast has reached the limit of its alcohol tolerance and cannot convert the remaining sugar. Most yeasts can ferment up to about 14 per cent alcohol, although a few can do better than this if the conditions are just right. If this is the cause of the fermentation stopping, then you will either have to drink the oversweet wine or blend it with one that is too dry.

If too much sugar is not the cause and fermentation still fails to resume, then the cause is probably due to the dying off of a weak yeast colony. Activate a fresh yeast in a starter bottle and, when it is fermenting well, add an equal quantity of stuck must to the starter and transfer it to a larger bottle. When this quantity is fermenting well add another equal volume of the stuck must and again transfer the fermentation to a still larger container. Repeat this process until all the stuck must has been added to the fermentation. Adding a fresh yeast to a stuck must rarely starts a fermentation. You must add it to the fermenting yeast in small doses and then only when the last dose is fermenting well.

Prolonged fermentation A very strong wine can be made in a somewhat similar manner. Begin the fermentation in the usual way and slowly add more and more sugar over a period of time so that the tolerance of the yeast can be gradually built up. Tokay and Madeira yeasts are the most tolerant, followed by sherry and port. When adding the sugar, remove some of the must, stir in the sugar and, when it is dissolved, return the sweetened must to the jar and the excess to the bottle. Pour the must slowly so as not to cause foaming. Stand the jar and bottle on a tray or in a polythene (plastic) bag in case there is any overflow during the fermentation. Indeed, this is sound advice for all fermentations.

Use the hydrometer frequently during a prolonged fermentation to ensure that the sugar is not added too soon. Wait until the specific gravity has fallen, say, to 1.006, and then add enough sugar to raise it, say, ten units to 1.016. When the gravity again falls to 1.006 repeat the process and so on. In this way one can produce a wine with the maximum amount of alcohol— up to 18 per cent and then sweeten it to taste. It is always preferable to add sugar to suit your taste rather than to have to drink a wine that is too sweet.

Such a prolonged fermentation needs plenty of acid and nutrient as well as an even temperature around 68°F/20°C. The addition of an extra teaspoonful/5 ml of citric acid and half that quantity of nutrient is therefore a wise precaution.

Stopping the fermentation Sometimes a sweet, low-alcohol wine of, say, 12 per cent is wanted. This can be achieved in two ways: by sweetening a dry wine of 12 per cent with lactose or saccharin or, alternatively, fermentation can be terminated when the wine still contains some sugar. To do this, move the jar to a cool place for a few days to slow down the fermentation and encourage the settling of the sediment, then siphon the clearing wine into another jar containing a 1 g tablet of potassium sorbate and a Campden tablet. Fermentation will stop almost immediately and the wine will be ready for the next stage.

Fermentation can also be stopped by chilling the wine, and siphoning it into a jar containing two crushed Campden tablets and some wine finings. As soon as the wine clears, rack it again and add one more Campden tablet.

Maturation

When fermentation is completely finished, the wine must be removed from the sediment of dead and living yeast cells, particles of pulp, protein, enzymes, bicarbonates, tartrates, and so on. Failure to do this results in a wine smelling and tasting of rotting vegetation. It is undrinkable.

The simplest way to remove the clearing wine from the sediment is to siphon it off, commonly called 'racking' the wine. Never pour the wine out through the bung-hole. Place the jar to be emptied on a table and the jar to be filled on the floor. Insert one end of the siphon into the wine and, if you wish, fix it firmly with the aid of a bored bung cut into two through the diameter of the bored hole. A narrow additional vent hole is needed so that air can replace the wine as it is removed. Place the halves of the bung around the siphon tube and fit the bung and tube into the neck of the jar. Push the tube to the appropriate level, suck the other end to fill it with wine, then place that end into the jar on the floor. The wine will flow steadily until the upper jar is emptied. By careful tilting of the upper jar, almost all the wine can be removed without disturbing the sediment. Or use a J-tube or blocked-end siphon (see page 32). Top the clean jar up with wine from the excess bottle, add a Campden tablet to protect it from infection and oxidation, bung tight, label and store in a cool place.

If the racking has been well done there will be nothing but sediment in the fermentation jar. This must be discarded and the jar washed out, drained dry and put away. Similarly the wine

from the excess bottle can be poured or siphoned into a smaller bottle and that sediment can also be washed out. If the racking has left some wine in the jar it can all be poured into the bottle. Replace the cotton wool plug and stand the bottle in the refrigerator. After a few days the wine will be clear and can be transferred to a clean bottle.

Should the wine remain hazy after a few months, proprietary wine finings may be added. Remove some of the wine from the jar and slowly pour it into the finings, stirring well all the time. When the finings are well mixed in, return the wine to the jar and stir well to distribute the finings evenly throughout the wine. Replace the bung and leave the jar in a cool place for a few days or a week. As soon as the wine is clear, rack it from the sediment, top up the jar, bung tight and store until it is ready for bottling.

Most wines mature best in bulk, but a period of bottle storage is also of value. Just how long a wine must be matured depends on the individual wine. In general, dry wines light in alcohol mature fairly quickly and strong sweet wines mature fairly slowly. **Every country wine needs at least six months from the time it is made to when it is first served; some need from two to three years.** You can only tell by tasting the wine and by experience. All too often, however, the best bottle is the last and you will wish that you had not drunk the others so soon!

Other wines

Sherry-type wines Sherry-type wines are matured slightly differently from other types of wine. They must be stored in jars about seven-eighths full that are plugged with cotton wool rather than with a bung. The plug filters out any microbes but permits the entry of air into the head-space above the maturing wine. Ferment on as strong as possible so that the alcohol content of the wine is appropriate to the oxidation necessary to obtain the characteristic nutty sherry flavour. Sherry-type wines are best matured dry and sweetened subsequently if so desired.

Sparkling wines Sparkling wines are best made from a light-flavoured still wine that is also light in alcohol—say, 10 to 11 per cent. When the wine is star bright and about six months old, rack it into a clean jar and stir in 2½ oz/70 g (⅓ cup) of caster (superfine) sugar per Imperial gallon/4.5 litres (5 quarts). (This quantity is critical and should not be exceeded or reduced.) Next, add an activated Champagne wine yeast and a little nutrient. Finally, fit an airlock and move the jar to a warm position for a few hours until the wine can clearly be seen to be fermenting.

Wash and sterilize six sparkling wine bottles (no others are suitable since they may be unsafe due to the pressure that builds in the bottle) and pour the fermenting wine into the bottles, leaving a headspace of 2 in/5 cm. Fit a softened, hollow-domed plastic stopper or a blister stopper to each bottle and wire it on with a cage (muselet). Leave the bottle on its side in a warm room, say, 68°F/20°C, for one week while the sugar is fermented, then move it to a cool place and keep it for at least six months, preferably longer, before disgorging the sediment.

Sediment will have deposited along the bottom side of the bottle, and this must be shaken down into the stopper or blister. To do this, place the bottles, head first, into a bottle carton set at an angle of 45 degrees. Each day, give the bottles a slight shake and twist, slowly moving the bottle round and round until the sediment has settled in the stopper or blister.

Make up a solution of one dozen ice cubes, well crushed, and 2 tablespoonfuls/30 ml of cooking salt. Stand the bottles, head down, in the ice for about 10 minutes to freeze the wine and the sediment in the stopper. Remove the cage, extract the stopper, quickly add one or two saccharin pellets and insert a clean and softened stopper. Replace the cage and store the wine for a few weeks or months longer. It helps if the wine in the bottle is first chilled (upside down, of course) for some hours in the refrigerator, since this inhibits the release of the carbon dioxide. It also helps if you handle the bottle carefully without shaking it and thus disturbing the carbon dioxide.

If blister stoppers have been used, seal the blisters with the wires provided and bend them down in accordance with the instructions.

Gooseberries, pears, rhubarb, white currants, and elderflowers all make splendid sparkling wines using this method.

Fortified wines Port or sherry-type wines can be fortified with additional spirit at the end of fermentation, after it has been racked and when the wine is bright. Vodka is the best spirit to add since it is colourless and tasteless, and thus will not affect the appearance or flavour of the wine. How much spirit to add can be calculated with the aid of a Pearson square as follows:

$$A \qquad\qquad B$$
$$C$$
$$D \qquad\qquad E$$

In the corner marked A write the alcohol content of the spirit that you propose to use, say, vodka at 40 per cent. In the corner marked B write the approximate alcohol content of the wine that you want to fortify, say, 14 per cent. In the centre marked C write the alcohol content that you wish to attain, say, 18 per cent. In the corner marked D write the difference between C and B (18−14=4). In the corner marked E write the difference between A and C (40−18=22). The proportion between D and E is the quantity of spirit to add to your wine. To increase the alcohol content in this example 4 parts of vodka at 40 per cent must be added to

22 parts of wine at 14 per cent to increase the alcohol content of the wine from 14 to 18 per cent. Or to put it another way, one bottle of vodka to 5½ bottles of wine.

The alcohol content of bottles of spirit is usually described as so many degrees proof, for instance 70° proof. You can convert this figure to percentage alcohol by dividing by 7 and multiplying by 4. (Maximum degrees proof is 175 and maximum percentage alcohol is 100; divide each by 25 and you have the ratio 7 to 4, so 7° proof equals 4 per cent alcohol and hence 70° proof equals 40 per cent alcohol.) In the United States proof is double the alcohol content, thus 80° proof equals 40 per cent alcohol.

Blending No matter how much care you take in making wine, occasionally the result is not quite as pleasing as you would like it to be. There may be nothing wrong with the wine itself but perhaps the fruit was too sour, or maybe insufficient acid was added to a flower must, or perhaps the wine is too sweet, or the flavour simply lacks appeal. Do not discard such wines. As long as the smell and taste is clean and free from infection, then the wine can be blended with another. Almost all commercial grape wines are blended to harmonize the flavour, but country winemakers all too often 'see their geese as swans'.

Blending emphasizes the best in wines and diminishes the worst. Bland wines develop character and new flavours are created. Simply pour the wines to be blended into a large bin, give them a gentle stir and return the blended wine to the jars. Sometimes fermentation starts again, so it is as well to fit an airlock to each jar after the wines have been blended. A new deposit is often thrown as well. Leave the blend for about a month to homogenize, then bottle it and think of a suitable name to describe it. That can be almost as enjoyable as the blended wine itself! All wines blend with one another. Sometimes a thin, flower wine can improve a vegetable or cereal wine dramatically.

Faults and Remedies

The most common fault of country wines in the past was that they were excessively sweet through using too much sugar. Wines were also unbalanced by having too much added alcohol. They often had a poor flavour, due to failure to use yeast or lack of proper hygiene. With better sugar control, the use of good wine yeast, and proper attention to hygiene through Campden tablets and a sulphite solution, these faults have been virtually eliminated. Nevertheless, occasionally something goes wrong, usually through carelessness in one way or another. Every fault can be prevented. The following list will help you pinpoint problems and—more important—rectify them.

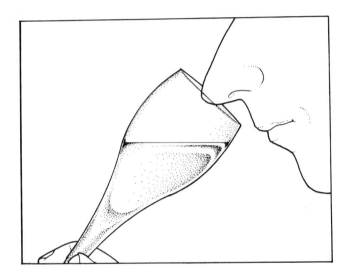

Oversweet This may be due to a poor fermentation, to too much sugar or to a failure to appreciate how much sugar there was in the fruit. Remember that the amount of sugar recommended in the recipe is only a guide and a more precise amount can be calculated with the aid of an hydrometer. If the wine is too sweet to drink, make a similar wine without sugar and blend the two together at the *start* of fermentation.

Too dry Add one or two saccharin tablets per bottle. This just takes the edge off the dryness and improves the flavour without making the wine taste sweet.

Medicinal taste This is due to insufficient acid. It may not be too late to stir in some citric acid. Try a few grains or more in a glass of wine. If it improves, add a proportionate amount to the whole.

Lacks character Probably due to insufficient tannin. Add a few drops of liquid tannin to a bottle of wine and if this is improved add the appropriate quantity to the whole. A level tea-spoonful/5 ml of grape tannin powder or liquid to an Imperial gallon/4.5 litres (5 quarts) is usually right for red wines.

Lacks bouquet and flavour Probably due to insufficient acid and poor quality ingredients. If the wine is otherwise sound, blend it with a wine too pronounced in smell and taste.

Hazy wine May be due to pectin from fruit and failure to use sufficient (or any) pectic enzyme. Pour a teaspoonful/5 ml of hazy wine into a tablespoonful/15 ml of methylated spirits. Shake well and leave for an hour. If strings or clots appear, the cause is pectin. Add a strong dose of pectolytic enzyme to the wine and leave in a warm place for twenty-four hours.

Haziness could also be due to suspended solids. Stir in a proprietary brand of wine fin-ings, in accordance with the instructions sup-plied with it, and leave the wine in a cool place for a few days. Apple wines often contain sus-pended protein. Stir in 2 fl oz/50 ml (¼ cup) fresh milk per Imperial gallon/4.5 litres (5 quarts). The wine should clear in twenty-four hours or so in a cool place.

Cereal and some vegetable wines can contain a starch haze. Check by placing a tablespoon-ful/15 ml of wine in a white saucer and add a few drops of household iodine. If the wine darkens, the cause is starch. Add fungal amylase as directed on the packet.

When hazy wines clear, rack into sterilized containers and add one Campden tablet per Imperial gallon/4.5 litres (5 quarts). If filtering becomes necessary add a half teaspoonful/2.5 ml grape tannin with the Campden tablet.

Rotten cabbage smell Due to leaving the wine on its sediment for too long. The sediment has decomposed and tainted the wine. No known remedy; discard the wine and sterilize the jar.

Vinegary smell and taste If only faint, add two Campden tablets per Imperial gallon/4.5 litres (5 quarts). This will prevent further deterioration. If pronounced add two Imperial pints/1.2 litres (5 cups) vinegar and provide access to warmth and air so that the wine will be totally converted to vinegar (see page 160).

Pear drop smell Caused by lack of nutrient for the yeast. No known remedy. Not likely to occur in fruit wines but possible in other wines if some grapes, whether fresh or dried or in the form of concentrated juice, are not included, or if nutrient salts are omitted.

Bitter almond smell Due to prussic acid from the inclusion of fruit stones (pits) and especially from their kernels. No known remedy. Exclude all large stones (pits) from the must and be sure not to cut or crack small pips and seeds.

Geranium smell Caused by using potassium sorbate alone to terminate fermentation with-out also adding sodium metabisulphite to pre-vent bacterial infection. No known remedy. Always add one Campden tablet per Imperial gallon/4.5 litres (5 quarts) when adding potassium sorbate.

Bad egg smell Caused by hydrogen sulphide made by the yeast unable to find sufficient pantothenic acid in the must. This is a member of the vitamin B_1 group and is needed more by some yeasts than others. No known remedy. Use good quality wine yeast and add the appropriate vitamin to non-fruit wines.

Mousey smell Due to bacterial infection. No known remedy; discard the wine and sterilize the container. Only occurs in low acid wines that have not been adequately sulphited when racked at the end of fermentation.

Oily appearance Due to bacterial infection. Pour the wine into a bin and beat it thoroughly with a wooden spoon or whisk to break up the ropes of bacteria. Add two crushed Campden tablets and return the wine to a sterilized jar. Leave in a cool place and, as soon as the wine looks normal, rack it from the sediment that has formed. The wine is safe to drink.

Re-fermentation Sometimes a wine starts to re-ferment about a year after being made. This is caused by bacteria converting the malic acid in the wine into lactic acid and carbon dioxide. The sharp flavour is ameliorated and the wine improved to some extent. But corks could pop and wine could be wasted. This malo-lactic fermentation can be prevented by sulphiting the wine after fermentation.

Sulphurous smell Due to the addition of too much metabisulphite. It can be caused by adding an uncertain quantity of loose metabisulphite to a wine. Campden tablets add a precise and known quantity—up to three tablets per gallon/4.5 litres (5 quarts) is unlikely to cause any smell of sulphur.

Countryside Recipes

Fruits, vegetables, flowers – even trees and their sap – have long been staple ingredients for the country winemaker. Herbs, grains and spices, although they often lack body and acid, can also be adapted into satisfying wines by using natural additives to provide the elements lacking in just a single ingredient. Many of the early recipes for country wines included sultanas and raisins, and even today, with the advent of commercial yeast and more scientific methods of winemaking, many winemakers still automatically add some fresh or dried grapes or concentrated grape juice to their wines in order to improve the flavour and aid the fermentation.

Of course not all grapes make good wine, and indeed most of the best wines in the world are made from a careful blend of different varieties of one species, *Vitis vinifera*. Certainly, many other fruits make excellent wines – far better ones than those made from poor grapes. The principle of blending is an important one in all forms of winemaking, and many country wines can be improved by using a mixture of different sub-varieties of fruit. Orange wine, for example, is best made from a blend of Seville and navel oranges, rose wine from the blooms of different species of rose, and so on.

Whichever recipes you embark on, it is as well to read the preparatory sections on equipment and ingredients – and especially winemaking methods – both before and during recipe testing. Each recipe can be tackled in isolation to some extent, but methods are not described in detail each time.

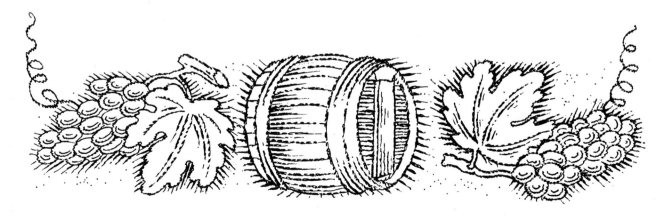

Fruit Wines

For many years there has been controversy about the methods of making fruit wines. Some winemakers use hot water to soften the fruit and extract the vital substances, others prefer to use cold water and a longer steeping. They argue that the hot water volatilizes some of the elements and so diminishes the flavour, and that the hot water gives a 'cooked' taste to the wine. In spite of such arguments, however, there are still some winemakers who actually boil the fruits until they are tender—even mushy, in the case of some fruits! They believe that they obtain the best extraction and, of course, pasteurize the juice at the same time.

Modern technology now provides us with an electric machine that blends the fruit for us without loss of anything. For small quantities of many fruits this method is undoubtedly best. Scientists in Australia have developed a heat treatment system, described in detail on page 21, which makes the best of both hot and cold methods. This system is particularly effective for elderberries, blackberries, bilberries, blackcurrants, damsons and black plums. Excellent colour extraction is obtained, the young wine is less harsh and it matures more quickly. The final flavour is clean, free of any stewed flavour and more redolent of the actual fruit. Volatiles do not appear to have been lost, for both aroma and bouquet are good.

Methods of 150 years ago left the fruit soaking for up to three weeks, unprotected by sulphite. It is difficult to imagine that the resultant wine could have been free from 'off' flavours and perhaps the great sweetness of the wines masked these horrors. Luckily our knowledge and technology are greater now, and the recipes which follow make use of modern techniques to produce sound, clean, enjoyable wines every time. Very occasionally, the resultant wine may not be quite up to your expectations, but this will be due to the quality of the fruit used, rather than to the method followed, provided you have faithfully followed the rules of hygiene set out in the previous chapters.

Always use the best quality fruit that you can get. Frozen fruit may be used to make wine in exactly the same way as fresh fruit. Indeed, it is sometimes advantageous to freeze hard fruits for forty-eight hours before making wine from them, since this softens them upon thawing and improves the juice extraction. It is important to sulphite them thoroughly before freezing, however, since they are inclined to oxidize during the thawing period. Large fruits, such as apples, pears and quince should be quartered before sulphiting and freezing them.

Dried fruits, too, may be used to make wine. Indeed, dried grapes in the form of sultanas and raisins make valuable additives to every must. Dried apricots, also make an excellent additive, contributing body and flavour. Figs, dates, prunes and rosehip shells produce excellent sherry-type wines. Dried elderberries, sloes and bilberries should be thoroughly washed in a sulphite solution before use since they are more prone to infection than those fruits with a high sugar content. They also tend to produce a rather brown/red wine instead of the clear red from the fresh fruit.

Bottled and canned fruits make excellent fast-maturing light wines, so do pure jams free from preservatives and added pectin. Bottled, canned, or cartoned, unsweetened fruit juices can also make attractive wines.

Fruits blend together exceptionally well and often produce even better wines than when used on their own—blackberry and apple is one particularly popular mixture.

Autumn Harvest Wine

Sometimes the quantity of any one fruit available is not enough to make a wine from it. The recipe which follows takes cognisance of this fact and makes use of many different fruits and vegetables. It is not essential to use every one of the ingredients mentioned below, nor in the specific quantities indicated. The recipe is intended as a guide to the possibilities open to you rather than as a precise instruction to follow without deviation. Keep the total weight of ingredients to between 6 and 6½ lb/2.75 and 3 kg, and try to maintain a balance between sharp tasting and bland ingredients. Serve Autumn harvest wine, free from chill, as an after-dinner wine.

Yield: 6 to 7 bottles

Imperial/metric	American
2 lb/900 g mixed cooking and eating apples	2 lb mixed cooking and eating apples
1 lb/450 g elderberries	1 lb elderberries
1 lb/450 g blackberries	1 lb blackberries
1 lb/450 g damsons	1 lb damsons
½ lb/225 g sloes	½ lb sloes
½ lb/225 g old runner beans	½ lb green beans
½ lb/225 g beetroot	½ lb beets
½ lb/225 g rose hips	½ lb rose hips
2 lemons	2 lemons
2 ripe bananas	2 ripe bananas
½ lb/225 g raisins	½ lb raisins
6 pints/3.5 litres water	7½ pints water
1 tsp/5 ml tartaric acid	1 tsp tartaric acid
1 tsp/5 ml pectic enzyme	1 tsp pectic enzyme
3 lb/1.35 kg white sugar	6 cups white sugar
Port wine yeast and nutrient	Port wine yeast and nutrient
Campden tablets	Campden tablets

Sterilize all equipment as needed. Start your records.

Stalk, wash and crush the apples and berries, stone (pit) the damsons and sloes; trim, scrub and dice the beetroot (beets), wash and slice the beans; trim, wash and crush the rose hips. Thinly pare the lemons avoiding all white pith, and express and strain the juice. Peel and slice the bananas and wash and chop the raisins. As each ingredient is prepared, drop it into a large preserving pan containing the water and 1 crushed Campden tablet.

When all the ingredients are in the pan, cover and place it on a hot stove. With the aid of a kitchen thermometer, check the temperature from time to time and when 175°F/85°C is reached, hold this for 15 minutes then remove the pan from the heat and leave the contents to cool. Be careful not to let the temperature rise so high that the ingredients boil.

When the temperature falls to 86°F/30°C, stir in the tartaric acid, pectic enzyme and the lemon juice. Cover and leave overnight.

Strain out, press dry and discard the solids. Check the specific gravity. Stir in half the sugar, add the activated yeast and nutrient and pour the must into a fermentation jar and any excess into a bottle. (Remember that the rest of the sugar will occupy about ¾ pint/400 ml of space in the jar.) Fit an airlock to the jar and a plug of cotton wool to the neck of the bottle. Ferment at 68°F/20°C for about 10 days.

Remove some of the wine, stir in half the remaining sugar and, when it is dissolved, return it to the jar. Continue fermenting the must for a further 7 days, then stir in the last of the sugar in the same way as before and ferment out.

When fermentation finishes and the specific gravity remains constant, taste the wine and, if needs be, sweeten it slightly to suit your taste. If you add 110 to your original specific gravity and deduct the final reading then, by consulting the chart given on page 180 you can find out the approximate alcohol content of your wine. For instance; original specific gravity 1.020+110 [3 lb/1.35 kg (6 cups)] sugar; [final specific gravity 1.016]. The total fermentation of 114 units (1.130−1.016=114) will produce approximately 15.5 per cent alcohol. Your wine will therefore be sweet and strong as well as full bodied and well flavoured.

Move the wine to a cool place for a few days to encourage clarification, then siphon into a sterilized jar, add 1 crushed Campden tablet and top up with wine from the bottle. Bung tight, label and store for at least 2 years before bottling.

If you can resist the temptation to drink it, keep this wine in bottle for a further year or two. It will go on improving and will not deteriorate for many years.

Apple Wine

Serve this wine nicely chilled as a dry white table wine. It is superb with roast pork. Apple wine is one of the very best of the country wines and should be made in as large a quantity as you can manage!

Yield: 6 to 7 bottles

Imperial/metric	American
9 lb/4 kg mixed cooking and eating apples	9 lb mixed cooking and eating apples
1 tsp/5 ml pectic enzyme	1 tsp pectic enzyme
Campden tablets	Campden tablets
1 tsp/5 ml citric acid	1 tsp citric acid
1 gallon/4.5 litres water	5 quarts water
½ tsp/2.5 ml grape tannin (optional)	½ tsp grape tannin (optional)
Champagne wine yeast and nutrient	Champagne wine yeast and nutrient
1½-2 lb/700-900 g white sugar	3-4 cups white sugar

Sterilize all equipment as needed. Start your records.

Wash and crush the apples, or cut them into small pieces with a stainless steel knife. Remove and discard all bruised portions and maggot holes. Leave on the skin and core provided the pips are not broken or cut.

Drop the prepared apples into a mashing bin containing the pectic enzyme, 1 crushed Campden tablet, the citric acid and the water. Cover and leave for 24 hours. Next day, check the specific gravity, add the tannin, and activated yeast and nutrient. Ferment on the pulp for 5 days, keeping the fruit submerged.

Strain out the juice and press the apples dry, preferably in a fruit press. Discard the pulp. Stir in the sugar. Pour the must into a fermentation jar and any excess into a bottle. Fit an airlock to the jar and a plug of cotton wool to the neck of the bottle. Ferment out at a temperature of around 61°F/16°C.

Siphon the clearing wine into a sterilized jar, add 1 crushed Campden tablet, top up with wine from the bottle, bung tight, label and store until clear (about 8 weeks). If the wine is slow to clear, 2 tablespoons/30 ml of fresh milk, well mixed in, soon precipitates the haze. When the wine is bright, rack again and keep for at least 9 months before bottling. Bottle, seal and label.

Keep for 3 or 4 months before serving.

Variations: In the author's opinion, apple wine is improved by the inclusion of 1 oz/25 g sultanas with each 1 lb/450 g of apples. The apples should be of as many different varieties as possible, including eating, cooking and some crab apples, if obtainable. Some hard pears may also be included, and even a few quince. If you make several apple wines during the season as different varieties become ripe, blend all the wines together the following spring.

You can make an attractive deep rosé wine by including 2 lb/900 g of blackberries, 1 lb/450 g elderberries, or 2 lb/900 g stoned (pitted) black plums or damsons. Wash, crush and add them to the apples at the outset. Another attractive rosé wine can be made from the residual pulp of a 5 Imperial gallon (6 US gallons) brew of apple wine and the residual pulp of a 5 Imperial gallon/22 litre (6 US gallons) brew of a blackberry/elderberry blend. Mix the two not too hard pressed pulps together in a bin, add 1 lb/450 g washed and chopped sultanas and 2 gallons/9 litres (10 quarts) of cold water. Ferment on the pulp for a further 5 days (no more yeast is necessary), then strain out and press the pulp again. Stir 3½ lb/1.5 kg (7 cups) white sugar and 2 teaspoons/10 ml of citric acid into the must and ferment out under an airlock. Finish as already described. This produces 13 bottles of excellent wine after 6 months' maturation.

Finished apple wines of poor flavour, due to poor-flavoured apples, can be blended to advantage with any flower wine—elderflower in particular.

Blackberry Wine

One of the great traditional country wines, Blackberry wine is best made from wild berries. Gather only large, juicy fruits that are black and ripe. Serve at room temperature as a strong, sweet after-dinner drink.

Yield: 6 to 7 bottles

Imperial/metric	American
6 lb/2.7 kg blackberries	6 lb blackberries
¾ lb/350 g raisins	¾ lb raisins
1 gallon/4.5 litres water	5 quarts water
1 tsp/5 ml pectic enzyme	1 tsp pectic enzyme
Campden tablets	Campden tablets
2 tsp/10 ml citric acid	2 tsp citric acid
½ tsp/2.5 ml grape tannin	½ tsp grape tannin
Port wine yeast and nutrient	Port wine yeast and nutrient
3 lb/1.35 kg white sugar	6 cups white sugar

Sterilize all equipment as necessary. Start your records.

Stalk, wash and crush the berries. Wash and chop the raisins. Place the prepared berries and the water in a suitable container and heat to 176°F/85°C. Maintain the temperature for 15 minutes, then leave to cool. Strain out the berry pulp through a fine-meshed nylon bag and press the fruit dry. Discard the pulp. Add the raisins, the pectic enzyme, 1 crushed Campden tablet and the citric acid. Cover and leave for 24 hours.

Next day, check the specific gravity, add the tannin and activated yeast and nutrient. Ferment on the raisin pulp for 5 days keeping the raisins submerged.

Strain out the juice and press the raisins dry. Discard the raisin pulp. Stir in one-third of the sugar, pour the must into a fermentation jar and a bottle. Fit an airlock to the jar and a plug of cotton wool to the bottle and continue the fermentation. Stir in half the remaining sugar 1 week later and repeat the process with the last of the sugar after a further week—then leave to ferment out.

Siphon the clearing wine into a sterilized jar, add 1 crushed Campden tablet, top up with wine from the bottle, bung tight, label and store. As soon as the wine is bright, rack again.

Store this wine in bulk for at least 1 year and preferably 2. Then bottle and store for a further 6 months. If you wish, you can sweeten the finished wine to your taste when decanting just before serving.

Variations: You can make this wine into a dry table wine by reducing the quantity of fruit and sugar by one-third and the acid by one-half. Make it in the same way but bottle when the wine is a year old.

Bilberries and blueberries may also be blended with blackberries.

Bilberry or Blueberry Wine

Fresh bilberries or blueberries are not widely available in the United Kingdom although they are quite common in both Australia and the United States. The wine which follows can be made from bottled bilberries (as here), or by equivalent quantities of fresh fruit. Serve as a dry red table wine.

Yield: 6 to 7 bottles

Imperial/metric	American
2 lb/900 g bottled bilberries, drained	2 lb bottled bilberries, drained
½ lb/225 g sultanas or concentrated red grape juice	½ lb golden raisins or concentrated red grape juice
6 pints/3.6 litres water	7½ pints water
Campden tablets	Campden tablets
2 tsp/10 ml citric acid	2 tsp citric acid
Burgundy wine yeast and nutrient	Burgundy wine yeast and nutrient
1¾ lb/770 g white sugar	3½ cups white sugar

Sterilize all equipment as needed. Start your records.

Empty the bilberries into a mashing bin and crush them with a potato masher. Wash and finely chop the sultanas (raisins).

Put the fruit, sultanas (raisins) or grape juice, water, citric acid, activated yeast and nutrient into a suitable container. Ferment on the pulp for 4 days, keeping the fruit submerged.

Strain and press the fruit dry. Discard the pulp. Measure the specific gravity. Stir in the right amount of sugar and pour the must into a fermentation jar and any excess into a bottle. (The must should fill the jar but, if necessary, top up with cold boiled water.) Fit an airlock to the fermentation jar and plug the neck of the bottle, if used, with cotton wool. Ferment out at around 68°F/20°C.

When fermentation is finished (about 3 weeks), siphon the clearing wine off the sediment into a sterilized jar. Add 1 crushed Campden tablet, store until bright, bung tight and label. As soon as the wine is bright, rack again. Mature in bulk for 6 months, then bottle. Keep for a further 6 months before serving.

Blackcurrant Wine

This is a fairly strong red social wine that you may need to sweeten slightly before serving.

Yield: 6 to 7 bottles

Imperial/metric	American
3 lb/1.35 kg blackcurrants	3 lb blackcurrants
½ lb/225 g raisins	½ lb raisins
1 gallon/4.5 litres water	5 quarts water
3 lb/1.35 kg white sugar	6 cups white sugar
Burgundy wine yeast and nutrient	Burgundy wine yeast and nutrient
Campden tablets	Campden tablets

Sterilize all equipment as needed. Start your records.

Stalk, wash and crush the blackcurrants. Wash and chop the raisins. Place the prepared blackcurrants and the water in a suitable container and heat to 176°F/85°C. Maintain the temperature for 15 minutes, then leave to cool.

Strain out the currant pulp through a fine-meshed nylon bag. Discard the pulp. Add the raisins and stir the sugar into the juice until it is dissolved. Add the activated yeast and nutrient and pour the must into a fermentation jar and any excess into a bottle. Fit the airlock into the jar and plug the bottle with cotton wool. Ferment out at around 70°F/21°C.

Siphon the clearing wine into a sterilized jar, add 1 crushed Campden tablet, bung tight, label and store until the wine is bright, then rack again.

Mature this wine in bulk for 1 year before bottling. Bottle and store for a further 6 months before drinking.

Damson Wine

Yield: 6 to 7 bottles

Imperial/metric	American
4 lb/2 kg ripe damsons	*4 lb ripe damsons*
1 gallon/4.5 litres water	*5 quarts water*
3 lb/1.35 kg white sugar	*6 cups white sugar*
Burgundy wine yeast and nutrient	*Burgundy wine yeast and nutrient*
Campden tablets	*Campden tablets*

Sterilize all equipment as needed. Start your records.

Wash, stalk and stone (pit) the damsons. Continue as described for *Blackcurrant wine*.

Variation: Add to the damsons 1 lb/450 g washed and chopped raisins and 4 ripe bananas. Use a Port wine yeast instead of a Burgundy yeast.

Prepare the must by heat treatment (see page 21) and strain it on to the washed and chopped raisins. When cool, measure the specific gravity. Add the yeast and ferment on the pulp for 5 days. Strain out and press the raisins. Stir in a teaspoonful/5 ml of citric acid, a teaspoonful/5 ml of grape tannin, and one-third of the sugar. Continue as described for *Blackberry wine*.

This wine needs to be stored at least 1 year in bulk and preferably longer. It also benefits from some bottle age. When it is fully mature, it is a rich, strong, sweet after-dinner wine.

Grape Wine

Wine from this fruit is best made from a blend of varieties: those made exclusively from one single variety are rarely as good as those made from a mixture. The following recipe is for a dry white table wine.

Yield: 6 to 7 bottles

Imperial/metric	American
18 lb/8 kg ripe white grapes	*18 lb ripe white grapes*
1 tsp/5 ml pectic enzyme	*1 tsp pectic enzyme*
Campden tablets	*Campden tablets*
White sugar as necessary	*White sugar as necessary*
All-purpose wine yeast and nutrient	*All-purpose wine yeast and nutrient*

Sterilize all equipment as needed. Start your records.

Stalk, wash and crush the grapes but not the pips. Place the crushed grapes in a suitable container with the pectic enzyme and 1 crushed Campden tablet. Cover and leave for 24 hours.

Next day, strain out the grapes and press dry. Discard the pulp. Measure the specific gravity of the juice. Add sufficient sugar to bring the reading up to between 1.076 and 1.090. Stir in an activated wine yeast and nutrient. Fit an airlock and ferment out at around 61°F/16°C.

When fermentation is finished, siphon off the wine from the sediment and add 1 crushed Campden tablet. Store until bright, then rack again and leave for a total of 6 months before bottling.

Store in the bottles for 3 months.

Variations: A red wine can be made from black grapes, either by fermenting on the pulp for 14 days or, better still, by using the heat treatment as described on page 21. Cool the grapes, strain, press and discard the pulp. When the liquor is cool, add the yeast and fit an airlock. Ferment out at a temperature of 68°F/20°C. Continue as for white wine, but mature in bulk for at least 18 months before bottling.

Previous page: Damsons mature into a strong after-dinner wine.

Mixed Fruit Wine 1

All the fruit used in this recipe are available at about the same time in summer. Mixed together in small quantities they make a most attractive rosé wine. Serve nicely chilled, with roast lamb, boiled potatoes and garden peas.

Yield: 6 to 7 bottles

Imperial/metric	American
½ lb /225 g blackcurrants	½ lb blackcurrants
1 lb /450 g redcurrants	1 lb redcurrants
1 lb /450 g white currants	1 lb white currants
½ lb /225 g raspberries	½ lb raspberries
½ lb /225 g strawberries	½ lb strawberries
½ lb /225 g Morello cherries	½ lb sour cherries
1 gallon /4.5 litres water	5 quarts water
1 tsp /5 ml pectic enzyme	1 tsp pectic enzyme
Campden tablets	Campden tablets
Bordeaux wine yeast and nutrient	Bordeaux wine yeast and nutrient
3 lb /1.35 kg white sugar	6 cups white sugar

Sterilize all equipment as needed. Start your records.

Stalk, wash, crush and stone (pit) the fruit. Put the crushed fruit, cold water, pectic enzyme and 1 crushed Campden tablet into a suitable container. Cover and leave for 24 hours.

Next day, measure the specific gravity, add the activated wine yeast and nutrient and ferment on the pulp for 3 days, keeping the fruit submerged and the bin loosely covered. Strain out, press dry and discard the fruit, stir in the sugar and fit an airlock.

When fermentation is finished, siphon the wine off its sediment into clean containers. Add 1 crushed Campden tablet and store until the wine is bright, then rack again.

Store the wine in bulk for 9 months, then bottle and store for 3 more. You can sweeten this wine slightly before serving if wished.

Mixed Fruit Wine 2

This recipe is for winter winemaking and is a fine example of making wines from canned fruits. It should be served young and fresh, nicely chilled.

Yield: 6 to 7 bottles

Imperial/metric	American
15½ oz /440 g can gooseberries	15½ oz can gooseberries
15½ oz /440 g can golden plums	15½ oz can golden plums
15½ oz /440 g can apricots	15½ oz can apricots
½ lb /225 g sultanas	½ lb golden raisins
7 pints /4 litres water	1 gallon plus 1½ cups water
1 tsp /5 ml pectic enzyme	1 tsp pectic enzyme
1 tsp /5 ml citric acid	1 tsp citric acid
Campden tablets	Campden tablets
All-purpose wine yeast and nutrient	All-purpose wine yeast and nutrient
2 lb /900 g white sugar	4 cups white sugar

Sterilize all equipment as needed. Start your records.

Open the cans, strain out and set aside the syrup in a cool place. Wash and chop the sultanas (raisins) and crush the canned fruit. Put all the fruit into a suitable container, cover with cold water, then add the pectic enzyme, citric acid and 1 crushed Campden tablet. Cover the container and leave for 24 hours.

Next day, add the fruit syrup, measure the specific gravity, then add the activated yeast and nutrient. Ferment on the pulp for 3 days, with the fruit submerged and the bin covered.

Strain out and drain the pulp dry without pressing, then discard it. Stir in the sugar, pour into a fermentation jar and fit an airlock. Ferment out at a temperature of 64°F/18°C.

When fermentation is finished, siphon the clearing wine off the sediment into a clean container, add 1 Campden tablet, top up with cold boiled water, if necessary, bung tight, label and store. As soon as the wine is bright, siphon it into sterilized bottles, seal and label.

Keep for 3 months before serving.

Variations: The separate ingredients all make excellent wines on their own: use three similar-sized cans of each.

Elderberry Wine

Undoubtedly the ingredient that makes the most popular of all country wines, the elderberry is sometimes referred to as the Englishman's grape. There are many different recipes, although the flavour of the fruit is so strong that many of the wines made from them taste much the same. Gather the elderberries from a number of separate bushes, selecting only the blackest berries. Pick them clean from their stalks excluding every trace of green and stem. Serve this sweet, strong, rich wine, free from chill, as an after-dinner drink.

Yield: 6 to 7 bottles

Imperial/metric	American
4½ lb/2 kg elderberries	4½ lb elderberries
1 lb/450 g ripe bananas	1 lb ripe bananas
1 lb/450 g raisins	1 lb raisins
2 lemons	2 lemons
2 oranges	2 oranges
1 gallon/4.5 litres water	5 quarts water
Port wine yeast and nutrient	Port wine yeast and nutrient
3 lb/1.35 kg white sugar	6 cups white sugar
Campden tablets	Campden tablets

Sterilize all equipment as needed. Start your records.

Wash and crush the elderberries. Peel and mash the bananas, wash and chop the raisins and thinly pare the rinds of the oranges and lemons, avoiding all white pith. Express and strain the citrus juice and set aside.

Put the crushed elderberries, citrus rinds, bananas, raisins and water in a boiling pan and heat to 176°F/85°C. Maintain this temperature for 15 minutes, then leave to cool. Strain into a suitable bin, pressing the fruit. Discard the pulp. Measure the specific gravity. Add the orange and lemon juice and the activated yeast and nutrient. Stir in one-third of the sugar and continue as described in the recipe for *Blackberry wine*.

Store in bulk for at least 2, possibly 3, years. Bottle and store for a further 6 months before drinking.

Note: Some recipes omit the bananas and raisins but this diminishes the richness of alcohol, body, flavour and vinosity of the finished wine. Since elderberries contain no acid worth mentioning, it is important to include the citrus fruit. Heating the elderberries in the manner described extracts all the glorious colour and flavour but avoids the bitterness so often found in elderberry wines made in other ways. Ensure that it does not boil.

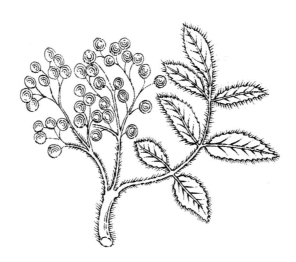

Orange Wine

There are many recipes for this very popular wine and everyone has his or her favourite: W. H. Roberts gives several in his book **The British Wine-maker and Domestic Brewer.** *Mrs Beeton also gives several in her classic cook book. Jane Austen made orange wine regularly. The following recipe is for a dry white wine which is excellent served cold with poultry, or as an aperitif.*

Yield: 6 to 7 bottles

Imperial/metric	American
5 sweet oranges	5 sweet oranges
5 bitter oranges	5 bitter oranges
1 gallon/4.5 litres of water	5 quarts water
½ lb/225 g sultanas or concentrated white grape juice	½ lb golden raisins or concentrated white grape juice
All-purpose wine yeast and nutrient	All-purpose wine yeast and nutrient
2¼ lb/1 kg white sugar	4½ cups white sugar
Campden tablets	Campden tablets

Sterilize all equipment as needed. Start your records.

Thinly pare the bitter oranges, avoiding all white pith. Chop the peel into small pieces, place it in a suitable container and pour 1 pint/550 ml (2½ cups) of hot water over it. Cover and leave to cool. Thinly pare the sweet oranges in the same way, lay the peel in a suitable container and place it in a cooling oven for a few minutes until it becomes golden brown. Remove from the oven and pour 1 pint/550 ml (2½ cups) of hot water over the peel, cover and leave to cool.

Wash and chop the sultanas (raisins), place them in a bin and pour the rest of the water on to them. Strain the liquor from the orange peels into the bin and discard the peels. Halve the oranges, express and strain the juice and add this to the bin, together with the activated wine yeast and nutrient. Ferment on the pulp for 4 days, keeping the sultanas submerged.

Strain out, press and discard the sultanas (raisins). Stir in the sugar, pour the must into a fermentation jar and any excess into a bottle. Fit an airlock to the jar and plug the neck of the bottle with cotton wool.

Ferment to a finish then siphon the clearing wine off the sediment into a clean container. Add 1 crushed Campden tablet, top up, bung tight and label. Store until the wine is bright, then rack again.

Store in bulk for 9 months, then bottle and keep for a further 3 months.

Variations: For a sweeter, satin-smooth fortified wine, increase the amount of sugar to 3 lb/1.35 kg (6 cups) and use a Sauternes yeast. Add a standard bottle of gin (a fifth) at the bottling stage and sweeten further to taste with saccharin.

For a fine, dry sherry-type wine, follow the same method but use 3 lb/1.35 kg (6 cups) of sugar and a sherry yeast. Add the sugar in three 'doses' to increase the alcohol tolerance of the yeast. If possible, ferment an additional ½ lb/ 225 g (1 cup) of sugar as well.

When fermentation is finished, mature the wine in containers not quite full so that there is a good surface area with access to the air. Use plugs of cotton wool instead of an airlock and bungs.

Orange Juice Wine

Serve this quick-maturing wine cold as an aperitif.

Yield: 6 bottles

Imperial/metric	American
1¾ pints/1 litre carton pure orange juice	1 quart carton pure orange juice
5¼ pints/3 litres cold water	6½ pints cold water
2 lb/900 g white sugar	4 cups white sugar
All-purpose wine yeast and nutrient	All-purpose wine yeast and nutrient
Campden tablets	Campden tablets

Sterilize all equipment as needed. Start your records.

Mix all the ingredients together and, when the sugar is dissolved, pour the must into a fermentation jar. Fit an airlock and ferment out to dryness.

Siphon the clearing wine off the sediment into a clean container. Add 1 crushed Campden tablet and, when bright, bottle, adding 1 saccharin tablet per bottle to take the edge off the dryness.

This wine matures quickly—store for 2-3 months before drinking.

Variations: Other unsweetened fruit juices, notably grapefruit, may be used in the same way.

Peach Wine

Some gardeners grow fan-trained peach trees against their garden walls and may well, therefore, have a surplus of fruit in certain years. Failing this, you can occasionally buy a whole tray of peaches for a reasonable price. For those able to obtain a supply of peaches, it is well worth making this sweet table wine. Serve chilled as a delightful accompaniment to the dessert course of a meal.

Yield: 6 to 7 bottles

Imperial/metric	American
4½ lb/2 kg ripe peaches	4½ lb ripe peaches
9 oz/250 g sultanas	9 oz golden raisins
6 pints/3.4 litres water	7½ pints water
½ oz/15 g citric acid	½ oz citric acid
1 tsp/5 ml pectic enzyme	1 tsp pectic enzyme
Sauternes wine yeast and nutrient	Sauternes wine yeast and nutrient
2¼ lb/1 kg white sugar	4½ cups white sugar
Campden tablets	Campden tablets

Sterilize all equipment as needed. Start your records.

Peel, stone (pit) and crush the peaches; wash and chop the sultanas (raisins). Put the fruit into a bin containing the water, citric acid, pectic enzyme and 1 crushed Campden tablet. Cover and leave for 24 hours. Add the activated yeast and nutrient and ferment on the pulp for 4 days, keeping the fruit submerged.

Strain out, press dry and discard the pulp. Stir in the sugar and, when it is dissolved, pour the must into a fermentation jar and any excess into a bottle. Fit an airlock to the jar and a plug of cotton wool to the neck of the bottle. Ferment out at around 64°F/18°C.

From time to time, check the specific gravity of the liquid and, when 1.016 is reached, rack the wine into a sterilized jar containing 1 g of potassium sorbate and 1 crushed Campden tablet. Seal the jar and store in a cool place.

When the wine is bright, rack again and store for 6 months before bottling. Keep for a further 3 months at least before serving, nicely chilled.

Gooseberry Wine

Gooseberries make some of the very best of the country white wines and you are strongly recommended to make as much wine from this fruit as you possibly can! There are many varieties suitable for winemaking and, if you possibly can, do make a wine from each separate variety and another from a mixture of all of them. The results are most interesting and you can derive great pleasure from comparison tasting. The recipe given below is for a dry white table wine.

Yield: 7 to 8 bottles

Imperial/metric	American
4 lb/1.8 kg just ripe gooseberries	4 lb just ripe gooseberries
1 gallon/4.5 litres boiling water	5 quarts boiling water
1 tsp/5 ml pectic enzyme	1 tsp pectic enzyme
Campden tablets	Campden tablets
3 lb/1.35 kg white sugar	6 cups white sugar
Bernkastel wine yeast and nutrient	Bernkastel wine yeast and nutrient

Sterilize all equipment as needed. Start your records.

Trim the gooseberries, wash them clean and place them in a polythene (plastic) bin. Pour the boiling water over the gooseberries, cover and set aside. When cool, drain off and save the water, and crush the now softened gooseberries with a potato masher or the like. Return the water, add a teaspoonful/5 ml of pectic enzyme and 1 crushed Campden tablet. Cover tightly and leave for 2 days.

Strain out and press the gooseberries dry, discarding the pulp. Measure the specific gravity. Stir in the white sugar, and add the activated yeast and nutrient. Pour the must into a fermentation jar and any excess into another container. The total quantity will be between 10 and 11 pints/5.5 and 6.2 litres (12.5 and 14 pints) and should produce 7 to 8 bottles of wine. Fit an airlock to each container and ferment out at a steady temperature of around 64°F/18°C.

When fermentation is finished, move the wine to a cool place for a few days and then siphon it into sterilized containers, dividing 1 crushed Campden tablet between them. Bung tight, label and store until the wine is bright, then bottle. This wine is best bottled early rather than matured in bulk.

Store the bottles for at least 1 year before serving. As the alcohol content is about 12 per cent, this wine will keep and improve for years. If necessary, sweeten it slightly to taste before serving. One saccharin tablet per bottle should be enough.

Variations: If you wish to make a sweeter, fuller wine, use 4½ lb/2 kg of fully ripe gooseberries and 3½ lb/1.5 kg (7 cups) sugar, together with a Sauternes yeast. Alternatively (a) use ½ lb/225 g sultanas instead of the extra sugar and sweeten to taste before serving: or (b) use ½ lb/225 g fructose instead of the extra sugar, or (c) use both the sultanas and the extra sugar or fructose. In this case terminate the fermentation when the specific gravity falls to 1.016 with 1 crushed Campden tablet and 1 g potassium sorbate or a proprietary brand of wine stabilizer.

The Sauternes yeast tends to produce more glycerine than other yeasts, especially in the presence of fructose which it finds more difficult to ferment. Hence this wine is richer and sweeter than other versions, although only a little stronger in alcohol.

Date Wine

This wine has a splendid brown robe but is best as a sweet sherry-type wine or Madeira-type wine rather than as a table wine. The rich brown sticky fruit contains much sugar but little acid. Serve free from chill after dinner, or between meals with Madeira cake.

Yield: 6 to 7 bottles

Imperial/metric	American
2¼ lb/1 kg dates	2¼ lb dates
½ lb/225 g raisins	½ lb raisins
2 lemons	2 lemons
1 bitter orange	1 bitter orange
1 grapefruit	1 grapefruit
7 pints/4 litres boiling water	8½ pints boiling water
Sherry or Madeira wine yeast and nutrient	Sherry or Madeira wine yeast and nutrient
2¼ lb/1 kg white sugar (brown for Madeira-type wine)	4½ cups white sugar (6 cups brown for Madeira-type wine)
Campden tablets	Campden tablets

Sterilize all equipment as needed. Start your records.

Stone (pit) and chop the dates; wash and chop the raisins. Thinly pare the lemons and orange, avoiding all white pith; express and strain the lemon, orange and grapefruit juice. Chop the lemon and orange rinds finely and place them in a bin with the dates and raisins. Pour over the boiling water, cover the bin and then leave to cool.

Add the lemon, orange and grapefruit juice to the bin, together with the activated yeast and nutrient. Ferment on the pulp for 5 days, keeping the fruit submerged.

Strain out and press the fruit dry. Discard the pulp. Stir in one-third of the sugar and pour the must into a fermentation jar and any excess into a bottle. Fit an airlock to the fermentation jar and plug the neck of the bottle with cotton wool. Ferment for 7 or 8 days.

Remove some of the wine, stir in half the remaining sugar and, when it is dissolved, return it to the jar. Continue fermenting the must for a further 7 or 8 days, then stir in the last of the sugar in the same way as before and ferment out.

Move the wine to a cool place for a few days to encourage clarification, then siphon into a sterilized jar, add 1 crushed Campden tablet and top up with wine from the bottle. Bung tight, label and store for at least 1 year before bottling.

Keep this strong sweet wine for a further 6 months in bottle before drinking.

Prune Wine

Good quality large prunes make a splendid sherry-type wine.

Yield: 6 bottles

Imperial/metric	American
2 lb/900 g prunes	2 lb prunes
7 pints/4 litres water	8¾ pints water
2 lb/900 g raisins	2 lb raisins
2 tsp/10 ml citric acid	2 tsp citric acid
Sherry wine yeast and nutrient	Sherry wine yeast and nutrient
2¼ lb/1 kg soft brown sugar	5 cups soft brown sugar

Sterilize all equipment as needed. Start your records.

Wash the prunes and soak them overnight in hot water. Next day, remove the stones (pits) and wash and chop up the raisins.

Add the raisins, citric acid and activated sherry wine yeast and nutrient to the prunes and liquid in which they were soaked. Cover loosely to allow the gas to escape and ferment on the pulp for 7 days, keeping the fruit submerged.

Strain out, press the fruit dry and discard the pulp. Measure the specific gravity. Stir in one-third of the sugar and continue as described for *Plum wine*.

Rosehip & Fig Wine

Fresh hips gathered from wild dog roses growing in the hedgerows, are used in this recipe. Alternatively, dried rosehip shells may be used. Figs have a very strong flavour and so must be used in great moderation. Both rosehips and figs are rich in vitamins and minerals and so add to the great popularity of this enjoyable sherry-type wine. Serve it chilled as an aperitif.

Yield: 6 bottles

Imperial/metric	American
4 pints/2.3 litres fresh rosehips or	5 pints fresh rosehips or
½ lb/225 g dried rosehip shells	½ lb rosehip shells
½ lb/225 g raisins	½ lb raisins
1 lemon	1 lemon
¼ lb/115 g dried figs	¼ lb dried figs
7 pints/4 litres water	1 gallon plus 1½ cups water
1 tsp/5 ml pectic enzyme	1 tsp pectic enzyme
3 tsp/15 ml citric acid	3 tsp citric acid
Sherry wine yeast and nutrient	Sherry wine yeast and nutrient
3 lb/1.35 kg Demerara or light brown sugar	7 cups light brown sugar

Sterilize all equipment as needed. Start your records.

Trim the fresh rosehips, rinse them in clean cold water and crush them. Wash and chop the raisins. Thinly pare the lemon rind, avoiding all white pith, express and strain the juice and set aside.

Place the crushed rosehips, lemon rind, figs (broken into small pieces) and water in a suitable container and heat to 176°F/85°C. Maintain the temperature for 15 minutes. Cover the pan and leave to cool. Strain the liquor on to the raisins and press and discard the pulp. Add the expressed and strained lemon juice, the pectic enzyme, citric acid and the activated sherry yeast and nutrient. Ferment on the raisin pulp for 5 days, keeping them submerged.

Strain out, press dry and discard the raisins. Stir in one-third of the sugar and continue the fermentation in the bin, loosely covered. Stir in the rest of the sugar in two equal doses at weekly intervals and leave to ferment out.

When fermentation is finished, siphon the clearing wine off its sediment into a sterilized storage jar and a large bottle, leaving a good headspace in both. Plug both containers with cotton wool and mature for 18 months, racking when a sediment is thrown and the wine is bright. Bottle, seal and label.

Overleaf: Rosehip and fig wine, rich in vitamins and minerals.

Gooseberry "Champagne"

Gooseberries also make a most delicious sparkling wine. The variety called 'Careless' is probably the best if you can obtain it, but any green type can be substituted. Drink the wine well chilled to enhance any festive occasion.

Yield: 6 bottles

Imperial/metric	American
3½ lb/1.5 kg green gooseberries	3½ lb green gooseberries
1 gallon/4.5 litres boiling water	5 quarts boiling water
1 tsp/5 ml pectic enzyme	1 tsp pectic enzyme
Campden tablets	Campden tablets
2½ lb/1.15 kg white sugar	5 cups white sugar
Champagne wine yeast and nutrient	Champagne wine yeast and nutrient
Caster sugar	Superfine sugar

Sterilize all equipment as needed. Start your records.

Trim the gooseberries, wash them and put them into a polythene (plastic) bin. Pour the boiling water over the gooseberries, cover and set aside. When cool, drain off and save the water and crush the now softened gooseberries with a potato masher or something similar. Return the water, add the pectic enzyme and 1 crushed Campden tablet. Cover tightly and leave for 2 days.

Strain out and press the gooseberries dry. Measure the specific gravity. Stir in the sugar, add an activated Champagne yeast and nutrient. Pour the must into a fermentation jar and any excess into a bottle. Fit an airlock to the container and a cotton wool plug to the neck of the bottle. Ferment out at a steady temperature of around 64°F/18°C.

When fermentation is finished, move the wine to a cool place for a few days and then siphon it into sterilized containers. Bung tight and store until the wine is bright then rack again.

When the wine is about 6 months old, rack into a sterilized container and stir in exactly 2½ oz/70 g (⅓ cup) of caster (superfine) sugar and another activated Champagne wine yeast and nutrient. Fit an airlock to the container and leave it in a warm place for several hours until the wine begins to ferment.

Carefully siphon or pour the fermenting wine into sterilized champagne bottles, leaving a 2 in/5 cm headspace at the top of each one. Fit a softened, hollow-domed blister or stopper to each bottle and wire on. Leave the bottles, on their side, in a warm place for 1 week.

Store the bottles, on their side, in a cool place for at least 6 months before drinking. Sediment will be deposited along the bottom of the bottle sides during storage and must be shaken down into the stopper or blister for removal. Please follow the instructions given for this procedure on page 43.

Rhubarb Wine

Red-stemmed, garden or field rhubarb is the ideal base for this wine. The red stalks impart a pinkish tinge to the wine. This recipe makes a medium dry table wine, best served cold with food appropriate to a white wine. Forced rhubarb and late rhubarb are not recommended.

Yield: 6 to 7 bottles

Imperial/metric	American
6 lb/2.7 kg rhubarb stalks	*6 lb rhubarb stalks*
1 orange	*1 orange*
3 lb/1.35 kg white sugar	*6 cups white sugar*
1 gallon/4.5 litres water	*5 quarts water*
All-purpose wine yeast and nutrient	*All-purpose wine yeast and nutrient*
Campden tablets	*Campden tablets*

Cut off the rhubarb leaves together with 1 in/2.5 cm top and bottom of the stalks. (This ensures that the stalk contains no unpleasant constituents such as oxalic acid.) Wipe each stalk with a clean cloth dipped in a sulphite solution made from half a Campden tablet and a pinch of citric acid dissolved in an additional cup of cold water. This removes most of the invisible moulds, fungi and bacteria as well as dust and soil, and makes the stalks really clean.

Sterilize all equipment as needed. Start your records. Crush, chop or mince (grind) the rhubarb stalks and place them in a polythene (plastic) bin together with the wiped, thinly pared and chopped up rind of the orange, devoid of all white pith. Cut the orange in half, express and strain the juice and set aside.

Place the orange rind and juice and one-third of the sugar in the bin containing the rhubarb. Pour on the cold water and stir well until the sugar is dissolved. Add the activated yeast and nutrient. Ferment on the pulp for 5 days. Keep the fruit submerged or press it down twice daily.

Strain out and press the fruit dry, discarding the pulp. Stir in the rest of the sugar and pour the must into a sterilized fermentation jar and the excess into a bottle. Fit an airlock to the jar and plug the neck of the bottle with cotton wool. Ferment out at a steady temperature of around 62°/17°C, or just a little lower.

When fermentation is finished, move the wine to a cold place for a few days, then siphon it off its sediment into a sterilized jar. Add a crushed Campden tablet, top up with wine from the bottle, label and store until the wine is bright. The small amount of wine left in the fermentation jar may be poured into the wine remaining in the bottle and, when the sediment has settled, the clear wine should be transferred to a bottle of a size that it will just fill.

Keep this wine for 1 year before drinking it. One glassful each day makes a splendid 'spring tonic'!

Note: The body and vinosity of this wine can be improved by adding ½ lb/225 g of washed and chopped sultanas (raisins) to the rhubarb.

Plum Wine

All the different varieties of plum make excellent wine. The skins of the red/black varieties lack colour and most wines made from them are rosé in colour. Golden plums and greengages make white table wines, while Victoria plums make a fine, sherry-type wine. Always use ripe plums to make wine.

Yield: 6 bottles

Imperial/metric	American
4½ lb/2 kg Victoria plums	4½ lb Victoria plums
½ lb/225 g sultanas	½ lb golden raisins
1 gallon/4.5 litres boiling water	5 quarts boiling water
1 tsp/5 ml pectic enzyme	1 tsp pectic enzyme
2 tsp/10 ml citric acid	2 tsp citric acid
Campden tablets	Campden tablets
Sherry wine yeast and nutrient	Sherry wine yeast and nutrient
3 lb/1.35 kg white sugar	6 cups white sugar

Sterilize all equipment as needed. Start your records.

Wash, stone (pit) and crush the fruit. Wash and chop the sultanas (raisins). Put the crushed fruit into a bin with the sultanas and pour over the water. Cover and leave it to cool. Add the pectic enzyme, citric acid and 1 crushed Campden tablet to the bin and then leave for 24 hours.

Add the activated yeast and nutrient and ferment on the pulp for 5 days, keeping the pulp submerged and the bin loosely covered.

Strain out, press dry and then discard the pulp. Stir in one-third of the sugar, cover loosely to allow the gas to escape, and continue fermentation in the bin for a further 1 week. Stir in half the remaining sugar and ferment as before for 1 week, then stir in the remaining sugar, and ferment.

Measure the specific gravity with a hydrometer and, when the reading is very low, say 1.002, add a further ½ lb/225 g (1 cup) of sugar if the fermentation is still proceeding. Try to finish the wine dry or nearly so.

Siphon the new wine off the sediment and add a crushed Campden tablet. Plug with cotton wool and leave to mature in containers not quite full.

Keep for at least 1 year before drinking, preferably longer.

Cherry Wine

Another enjoyable wine for social drinking.

Yield: 6 to 7 bottles

Imperial/metric	American
5 lb/2.25 kg cooking and Morello cherries, mixed	5 lb cooking and sour cherries mixed
1 gallon/4.5 litres water	5 quarts water
3 lb/1.35 kg white sugar	6 cups white sugar
Burgundy wine yeast and nutrient	Burgundy wine yeast and nutrient
Campden tablets	Campden tablets

Sterilize all equipment as needed. Start your records.

Wash, stalk and stone (pit) the cherries. Continue as described for *Blackcurrant wine*. This wine can be improved by adding 9 oz/250 g of sultanas (raisins).

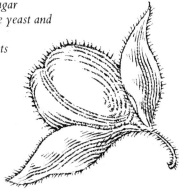

White Currant Wine

This fruit deserves to be more popular with winemakers. This particular recipe makes a good dry white table wine, which should be served chilled. White currants also make an excellent sparkling wine.

Yield: 6 bottles

Imperial/metric	American
3 lb/1.35 kg white currants	3 lb white currants
½ lb/225 g sultanas	½ lb golden raisins
7 pints/4 litres water	1 gallon plus 1½ cups water
1 tsp/5 ml pectic enzyme	1 tsp pectic enzyme
Campden tablets	Campden tablets
Chablis wine yeast and	Chablis wine yeast and
nutrient	nutrient
2lb/900g white sugar	4 cups white sugar

Sterilize all equipment as needed. Start your records.

Stalk, wash and crush the currants. Wash and chop the sultanas (raisins). Add the prepared fruit to the cold water, pectic enzyme and 1 crushed Campden tablet. Cover and leave for 24 hours.

Next day, measure the specific gravity. Add the activated yeast and nutrient and ferment on the pulp for 4 days, keeping the fruit submerged. Strain out, press and discard the fruit. Stir in the sugar and fit an airlock. Ferment out at around 61°F/16°C.

When fermentation is complete, siphon the wine into a clean storage container. Add 1 crushed Campden tablet.

Mature for 6 months before bottling as a table wine, or re-ferment as a sparkling wine by following the instructions given on page 43, or the recipe for *Gooseberry 'Champagne'* given on page 68.

Mixed Berry Wine

This traditional country wine makes a superbly rich social drink, served at room temperature.

Yield: 6 to 7 bottles

Imperial/metric	American
5 lb/2.5 kg blackberries	5 lb blackberries
½ lb/225 g blackcurrants	½ lb blackcurrants
2 ripe bananas	2 ripe bananas
½ lb/225 g raisins	½ lb raisins
1 gallon/4.5 litres water	5 quarts water
1 tsp/5 ml pectic enzyme	1 tsp pectic enzyme
Campden tablets	Campden tablets
2 tsp/10 ml citric acid	2 tsp citric acid
½ tsp/2.5 ml grape tannin	½ tsp grape tannin
Port wine yeast and nutrient	Port wine yeast and nutrient
3 lb/1.35 kg white sugar	6 cups white sugar

Sterilize all equipment as needed. Start your records.

Stalk, wash and crush the berries, blackcurrants and bananas. Wash and chop the raisins.

Place the prepared fruit (except the raisins), and the water in a suitable container and heat to 176°F/85°C. Maintain the temperature for 15 minutes. Leave to cool. Strain out the pulp through a fine-meshed nylon bag and press it dry. Discard the pulp. Add the pectic enzyme, 1 crushed Campden tablet and the citric acid. Cover and leave for 24 hours.

Next day, measure the specific gravity. Add the tannin and activated yeast and nutrient. Stir in one-third of the sugar and pour the must into a fermentation jar and bottle. Fit an airlock to the jar and a plug of cotton wool to the bottle and continue the fermentation.

After 1 week, remove half the wine from the jar, stir in half the remaining sugar and return the must slowly to the jar and the excess to the bottle. Repeat the process 1 week later and leave to ferment out.

Continue as described in *Blackberry wine*.

Mulberry "Madeira"

The purple-ripe berries of the mulberry tree make a delicious, rich sweet wine—particularly suitable for after-dinner drinks with cheese and biscuits.

Imperial/metric	American
6 lb/2.7 kg mulberries	6 lb mulberries
½ lb/225 g raisins	½ lb raisins
1 gallon/4.5 litres water	5 quarts water
1 tsp/5 ml pectic enzyme	1 tsp pectic enzyme
Campden tablets	Campden tablets
2 tsp/10 ml citric acid	2 tsp citric acid
½ tsp/2.5 ml grape tannin	½ tsp grape tannin
Madeira wine yeast and nutrient	Madeira wine yeast and nutrient
3 lb/1.35 kg Demerara or soft brown sugar	7 cups light brown sugar

Sterilize all equipment as necessary. Start your records.

Wash and crush the mulberries. Wash and chop the raisins. Place the prepared mulberries and raisins in the water in a suitable container and heat to 176°F/85°C. Maintain the temperature for 15 minutes. Leave to cool. Strain out the pulp through a fine-meshed nylon bag and press the fruit dry. Discard the pulp. Add the pectic enzyme, 1 crushed Campden tablet and the citric acid. Cover and leave for 24 hours.

Next day, measure the specific gravity. Add the tannin and activated wine yeast and nutrient. Stir in one-third of the brown sugar, pour the must into a fermentation jar and the excess into a bottle. Fit an airlock to the jar and a plug of cotton wool to the bottle and continue the fermentation.

After 1 week, remove half the wine from the jar, stir in half the remaining sugar and return the must slowly to the jar and the excess to the bottle. Repeat the process 1 week later and leave to ferment out.

Continue as described for *Blackberry wine.*

Strawberry Jam Wine

Strawberries lose much of their delicious flavour when made into wine. Dry fresh strawberry wine is particularly poor; a sweet wine is acceptable, but a much better wine can be made from strawberry jam. Use a full fruit, sugar and water only jam and avoid any containing added pectin, preservatives or colouring matter. (Home-made jam is probably the best.) The following recipe makes an attractive rosé wine with a strawberry flavour. It should be served nicely chilled.

Yield: 6 bottles

Imperial/metric	American
3 lb/1.35 kg strawberry jam	3 lb strawberry jam
7 pints/4 litres water	1 gallon plus 1¼ cups water
2 tsp/10 ml citric acid	2 tsp citric acid
2 tsp/10 ml pectic enzyme	2 tsp pectic enzyme
Campden tablets	Campden tablets
All-purpose wine yeast and nutrient	All-purpose wine yeast and nutrient
1 lb/450 g white sugar	2 cups white sugar

Sterilize all equipment as needed. Start your records.

Dissolve the jam in hot water and set aside. When the liquor is cool, add the citric acid, pectic enzyme and 1 crushed Campden tablet. Cover and leave for 24 hours.

Measure the specific gravity. Add the activated yeast and nutrient and ferment on the pulp for 5 days, then strain out the pulp and stir in the sugar. Pour the must into a sterilized fermentation jar and fit an airlock. Ferment out to dryness.

Siphon the new wine off the sediment into a sterilized jar and add 1 crushed Campden tablet. Store until the wine is bright, then rack it again.

Mature in bulk for 6 months then bottle, adding 1 saccharin tablet per bottle. It is then ready to drink.

Note: Other jams and jellies may be used in the same way.

Overleaf: Mulberry 'Madeira' and Strawberry Jam wine, two delicately coloured 'fruity' wines.

Vegetable Wines

Experience over the centuries shows that vegetables—like fruits and flowers—grow better in some soils and climates than others. Indeed, in some vegetable-growing areas, fruits are often scarce, and it was probably in such areas that early experiments were made with vegetables as a base for wine. As with fruits and flowers, some vegetables have produced more enjoyable wines than others. In the author's opinion, carrot and parsnip are best, although broad (fava) beans, celery, lettuce, mangold, marrow (squash) pea pods, potatoes, runner (green) beans and turnips all make acceptable wines.

Vegetables contain little acid or sugar but they do contribute body and nitrogenous matter as well as flavour. Frequently the flavour is quite light and spices, dried fruit and brown sugars are therefore often added.

Root vegetables should be scrubbed clean and never peeled, since much of the goodness lies in the skin. Surface vegetables must be washed clean. Vegetables are usually boiled until they are soft and tender, but not mushy. They are then strained out and discarded (or eaten) and the wine is made from the liquor. Both table and social wines can be made from vegetables.

The recipes that follow include dried grapes (raisins) since they add vinosity to the wine and provide additional nutrients for the yeast, thus helping to promote a more effective fermentation. Acid may be provided from citrus fruits or from crystals. The latter are cheaper and more precise but citrus parings often have a subtle effect on the flavour.

Most vegetable wines take a year or even two to reach their best and will keep for several years after that. It is worth using several half-size bottles to try first so that you can monitor the progress of the wine.

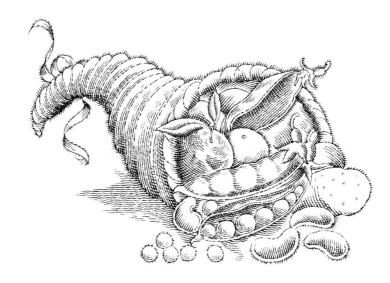

Broad (Fava) Bean Wine

This is a light, dry, white table wine, suitable for serving lightly chilled with fish, pork and poultry.

Yield: 6 to 6½ bottles

Imperial/metric	American
4½ lb/2 kg broad beans	4½ lb fava beans
3 lemons	3 lemons
½ lb/225 g sultanas	½ lb golden raisins
1 gallon/4.5 litres water	5 quarts water
1¾ lb/775 g sugar	3½ cups sugar
German wine yeast and nutrient	German wine yeast and nutrient
Campden tablets	Campden tablets

Sterilize all equipment as needed. Start your records.

Use old broad beans at the end of the season. Shuck them and discard the husks. Thinly pare the lemon rinds, avoiding all white pith. Express and strain the juice and set aside. Wash and chop the sultanas (raisins).

Boil the beans with the lemon rind and water for 1 hour. Strain the liquor through a nylon strainer into a polythene (plastic) bin containing the sultanas. Stir well, top up with cold water and cover the bin until the liquor is cool. Then add the lemon juice and activated wine yeast and nutrient.

Ferment on the pulp for 3 days, then strain out the sultanas. Stir in the sugar, pour the must into a fermentation jar, fit an airlock and ferment out.

Siphon the clearing wine off the sediment into a clean jar. Add 1 crushed Campden tablet. When the wine is bright, rack into bottles.

Store for 6 months.

Pea Pod Wine

This is a pleasant, white light table wine. Serve chilled with fish, pork or poultry.

Yield: 6 to 6½ bottles

Imperial/metric	American
4½ lb/2 kg young pea pods	4½ lb young pea pods
2 lemons	2 lemons
½ lb/225 g sultanas	½ lb golden raisins
1 gallon/4.5 litres water	5 quarts water
1¾ lb/770 g sugar	3½ cups sugar
German wine yeast and nutrient	German wine yeast and nutrient
Campden tablets	Campden tablets

Sterilize all equipment as needed. Start your records.

It is important to use very fresh young pea pods as soon as they have been shucked. Boil them until soft and tender with the thinly pared lemon rinds and as much of the water as your boiling pan will hold, up to 1 gallon/4.5 litres (5 quarts). Wash and chop the sultanas (raisins). Express and strain the lemon juice and set aside.

Pour the liquor through a nylon strainer into a polythene (plastic) bin containing the sultanas (raisins) and sugar. Discard the pea pods and rind. Stir well, top up with cold water and cover the bin until the liquor is cool. Then add the lemon juice and activated yeast and nutrient.

Continue as described for *Broad (fava) bean wine.*

Beetroot (Beet) Wine

This wine has a magnificent colour, and is strong and sweet. Serve it at room temperature as an after-dinner drink.

Yield: 6 to 6½ bottles

Imperial/metric	American
5 lb/2.25 kg beetroots	5 lb beets
3 large lemons	3 large lemons
1 lb/450 g raisins	1 lb raisins
1 gallon/4.5 litres water	5 quarts water
Port wine yeast and nutrient	Port wine yeast and nutrient
3 lb/1.35 kg sugar	6 cups sugar
Campden tablets	Campden tablets

Sterilize all equipment as needed. Start your records.

Choose freshly dug beetroots (beets). Trim them, scrub them clean and cut into small, dice-sized pieces. Thinly pare the lemon rinds, avoiding all white pith. Express and strain the lemon juice and set it aside. Wash and chop the raisins.

Place the beetroot (beets) in a boiling pan with the lemon rinds. Add enough water comfortably to fill the pan, cover it, bring to the boil and simmer for up to 1½ hours until the beetroot (beet) is soft to the fork. Strain the liquor through a nylon strainer or bag into a polythene (plastic) bin containing the raisins. Top up to the required level, cover the bin and leave the liquor to cool. Then measure the specific gravity and add the lemon juice and activated yeast and nutrient.

Ferment on the raisin pulp for 5 days, keeping the raisins submerged. Strain out, press and discard the raisins. Stir in one-third of the sugar and fit an airlock. Ferment for about 7 days. Remove half the wine, stir in another third of the sugar and return the fermenting must to the jar and the accompanying bottle. About a week later, repeat the process with the last of the sugar and continue the fermentation.

Siphon the clearing wine off the sediment into a clean jar and top up with the wine from the bottle. Add 1 crushed Campden tablet, bung tight, label and store. Pour the residue from the jar into the bottle and, as soon as the sediment settles, pour the clean wine into another bottle that it can just fill.

Mature this wine for 1 year in bulk. Bottle and store for another 1 year before drinking.

Celery Wine

This attractive white table wine can be served chilled with baked fish, pork or poultry. It was once thought to be a remedy for rheumatism.

Yield: 6 to 6½ bottles

Imperial/metric	American
4½ lb/2 kg celery	4½ lb celery
2 lemons	2 lemons
½ lb/225 g sultanas	½ lb golden raisins
1 gallon/4.5 litres water	5 quarts water
2¼ lb/1 kg sugar	4½ cups sugar
Burgundy wine yeast and nutrient	Burgundy wine yeast and nutrient
Campden tablets	Campden tablets

Sterilize all equipment as needed. Start your records.

Select large celeries in good condition. Cut off the leaves and roots, remove the stalks, wash them thoroughly and cut them into small pieces. Thinly pare the lemons, avoiding all white pith. Express and strain the juice and set aside. Wash and chop the sultanas (raisins).

Boil the celery, lemon parings and water together for 45 minutes. Strain out and continue as described for *Beetroot (beet) wine*.

Keep for at least 1 year before drinking.

Previous page: Beetroot (beet) produces a strong and richly coloured wine.

Marrow (Squash) Wine

This vegetable has very little flavour and the addition of some spice is therefore necessary. It produces a social wine excellent for drinking cold during the evening. Pumpkin may be substituted with advantage for marrow.

Yield: 6 to 6½ bottles

Imperial/metric	American
4½ lb/2 kg marrow	4½ lb squash
1 grapefruit	1 grapefruit
1 lemon	1 lemon
1 orange	1 orange
1 oz/25 g root ginger	1 oz ginger root
½ lb/225 g sultanas	½ lb golden raisins
1 gallon/4.5 litres boiling water	5 quarts boiling water
All-purpose wine yeast and nutrient	All-purpose wine yeast and nutrient
2¼ lb/1 kg white sugar	4½ cups white sugar
Campden tablets	Campden tablets

Sterilize all equipment as needed. Start your records.

Wipe the marrow (squash) and cut it up into dice-sized pieces, using the rind, pulp and seeds— but be careful not to cut the seeds. Place in a polythene (plastic) bin. Very thinly pare the citrus fruit, excluding all white pith. Express and strain the juice and set aside. Bruise the root ginger well. Wash and chop the sultanas (raisins).

Place the fruit parings, ginger and sultanas in the bin with the marrow (squash) and pour the water over them. Cover and leave to cool. Add the fruit juice and the activated wine yeast and nutrient. Ferment on the pulp for 5 days, keeping the fruit submerged.

Strain out, press and discard the pulp. Stir in all the sugar. Pour the must into a fermentation jar and any excess into a bottle. Fit an airlock to the jar and a plug of cotton wool to the neck to the bottle. Ferment out until finished.

Siphon the clearing wine off the sediment into clean bottles and continue as described for *Broad (fava) bean wine.*

Potato Wine

This is a strong sweet wine. Serve chilled as a social drink during the evening.

Yield: 6 to 6½ bottles

Imperial/metric	American
4½ lb/2 kg potatoes	4½ lb potatoes
2 lemons	2 lemons
2 oranges	2 oranges
½ oz/15 g root ginger	½ oz ginger root
1 gallon/4.5 litres water	5 quarts water
1 lb/450 g raisins	1 lb raisins
Madeira wine yeast and nutrient	Madeira wine yeast and nutrient
3 lb/1.35 kg light brown sugar	7 cups light brown sugar

Sterilize all equipment as needed. Start your records.

Use main crop potatoes if at all possible—new potatoes are not suitable. Scrub them well and cut into small dice-sized pieces. Thinly pare the lemons and oranges (Seville if available), avoiding all white pith. Express and strain the juice and set aside. Bruise the ginger.

Boil the potatoes, fruit parings, ginger and water together for 30 minutes—no longer. Strain the liquor on to the washed and chopped raisins and continue as for *Beetroot (beet) wine.*

Carrot Wine

This light table wine is delicious served slightly chilled.

Yield: 6 to 6½ bottles

Imperial/metric	American
4½ lb/2 kg carrots	4½ lb carrots
2 oranges	2 oranges
2 lemons	2 lemons
½ lb/225 g sultanas	½ lb golden raisins
1 gallon/4.5 litres water	5 quarts water
2¼ lb/1 kg white sugar	4½ cups white sugar
Burgundy wine yeast and nutrient	Burgundy wine yeast and nutrient
Campden tablets	Campden tablets

Sterilize all equipment as needed. Start your records.

Select good quality, freshly dug, main crop carrots. Wash, scrub and dice them. Thinly pare the oranges and lemons, avoiding all white pith. Express and strain the juice and set aside. Wash and chop the sultanas (raisins).

Boil the carrots, citrus rinds and water together for 30 minutes. Strain the liquor through a nylon strainer, into a polythene (plastic) bin containing the sultanas (raisins). Stir well, top up with cold water and cover the bin until the liquor is cool. Then add the lemon and orange juice and the activated yeast and nutrient. Cover the bin and ferment on the sultana pulp for 3 days.

Strain out the sultanas, stir in the sugar and pour the must into a sterilized fermentation jar. Fit the airlock and ferment out. Rack and store as described for *Beetroot (beet) wine*.

Keep for 1 year before drinking.

Parsnip Wine

One of the great traditional country wines. This particular recipe makes a golden dessert wine.

Yield: 6 to 6½ bottles

Imperial/metric	American
4½ lb/2 kg parsnips	4½ lb parsnips
2 lemons	2 lemons
2 oranges	2 oranges
1 lb/450 g raisins	1 lb raisins
1 gallon/4.5 litres water	5 quarts water
Madeira wine yeast and nutrient	Madeira wine yeast and nutrient
3 lb/1.35 kg light brown sugar	7 cups light brown sugar
Campden tablets	Campden tablets

Sterilize all equipment as needed. Start your records.

Use freshly dug parsnips. Scrub them clean and dice small. Thinly pare the lemon and orange rinds, avoiding all white pith. Express and strain the juice and set aside. Wash and chop the raisins.

Continue as described for *Beetroot (beet) wine*.

Mature for 1 year in bulk and up to another 1 year in the bottle.

Flower Wines

Despite the enormous range of fruits available, enthusiastic winemakers constantly seek new ingredients. Foremost among them are flowers. They contribute their fragrance, both in aroma and in flavour but, sadly, they have little else to offer, and all other ingredients must be added to provide the body, acid and alcohol necessary to make good wine.

Flowers should be picked when fully open, preferably early, on a dry and sunny day before the heat has robbed them of too much of their fragrance. Care should be taken in picking wild flowers, not to damage bushes or trees, or to dig up roots or totally denude an area. Bulb and tuberous rooted flowers should not be used for winemaking.

Dandelion, elderflower and rose petal remain the most popular of flower wines and are, therefore, described first. But some other flower wines are also worth making and so are included in this section.

All flower wines taste best as medium-sweet social wines drunk between meals. It is often best to ferment the wine out to dryness and to sweeten afterwards with saccharin at the bottling stage. Too much sugar will make the wine too strong and unbalanced where, ideally, it should be light and rather delicate.

Small packets of dried flowers suitable for making wine can be obtained from herbalists and some home brew shops. One small packet is enough to make six bottles.

Dandelion Wine

Traditionally, this wine should be made on St George's Day, 23 April. It can be sweet, medium or dry but tastes best when made as a medium sweet wine (as here). Although it can be served as a table wine, it shows to better advantage when served slightly chilled as a social wine. Coltsfoot flowers can be substituted for dandelions.

Yield: 6 to 6½ bottles

Imperial/metric	American
1 gallon/4.5 litres flower heads	5 quarts flower heads
1 orange	1 orange
2 lemons	2 lemons
½ lb/225 g sultanans	½ lb golden raisins
1 gallon/4.5 litres boiling water	5 quarts boiling water
All-purpose wine yeast and nutrient	All-purpose wine yeast and nutrient
2¼ lb/1 kg white sugar	4½ cups white sugar
Campden tablets	Campden tablets

Sterilize all equipment as needed. Start your records.

Collect the flowers and cut off the yellow heads, discarding every trace of green stem, leaf and calyx. Put the petals into a measuring jug and shake down gently: do not press. Pare the orange and lemons, making sure that all the white pith is discarded. Chop the rind. Express the juice of the orange and lemons, wash and chop the sultanas (raisins).

Put the petals into a plastic bin with the orange and lemon rinds and the sultanas (raisins). Pour over the boiling water, cover and cool. Stir in the orange and lemon juice, the activated yeast and nutrient, cover loosely and leave to ferment on the pulp for 5 days, pressing down the floating fruit and flowers twice daily.

Strain the pulp, pressing until all the juice is extracted. Discard the pulp. Stir in the sugar. Pour the must into a fermentation jar and any excess into a bottle. Fit an airlock to the fermentation jar and plug the bottle with cotton wool. Leave to ferment out at around 68°F/20°C. When fermentation is finished, move the wine to a cool place for a few days to help it to clear.

Siphon the clearing wine off the sediment into a sterilized jar. Add 1 crushed Campden tablet, top up the jar from the bottle, bung tight, label and store in a cool place. When the wine is bright, rack it again. Mature in bulk for 6 months before siphoning off into bottles.

Keep for 1 year before drinking, and sweeten to taste before serving.

Marigold Wine

The large, orange-coloured English marigold (or **Calendula** as it is more properly called) is the flower to use for this wine. Traditionally it was used as a remedy for heart weaknesses and was regularly made as a tonic wine by pre-Reformation monks, who provided much of the medical care available at that time. The flowers bloom during summer and autumn and may be gathered at any time provided they are fully open.

Yield: 6 bottles

Imperial/metric	American
5 pints/2.8 litres marigold flowers	6¼ pints marigold flowers
2 oranges (Seville if possible)	2 oranges (Seville if possible)
1 lemon	1 lemon
½ lb/225 g sultanas or raisins	½ lb golden raisins or raisins
1 gallon/4.5 litres water	5 quarts water
2¼ lb/1 kg white sugar	4½ cups white sugar
All-purpose wine yeast and nutrient	All-purpose wine yeast and nutrient
Campden tablets	Campden tablets

Sterilize all equipment as needed. Start your records.

Collect the flowers, strip off and discard the leaves, stems and calyx. Put them into a measuring jug and shake them down gently; do not press.

Pare the oranges and lemon, avoiding all white pith. Chop the rind and set it aside. Express and strain the juice, wash and chop the sultanas or raisins.

Put the flower heads into a plastic bin with the orange and lemon rinds and the sultanas or raisins. Pour over the boiling water and leave to cool. Stir in the orange and lemon juice and the activated yeast and nutrient, cover loosely and ferment on the pulp for 5 days, pressing down on the floating fruit and flowers twice daily.

Strain out the solids, pressing until all the juice is extracted. Discard the pulp. Stir in the sugar, then pour the must into a fermentation jar and any excess into a bottle. Fit an airlock to the fermentation jar and plug the neck of the bottle with cotton wool. Leave to ferment out at around 68°F/20°C.

When fermentation is finished, siphon the clearing wine off the sediment into a clean container, add 1 crushed Campden tablet and store until the wine is bright, then bottle.

Keep for 9 months or longer before drinking.

Elderflower Wine

Creamy-coloured elderflower florets grow in profusion on many branches from a single stalk on the elder bush. Gather them on a warm, sunny day when the florets are fully open. There are at least eight different varieties of elder and the best wine is made from a mixture of several varieties. The wine is white and medium-sweet and should be served slightly chilled.

Yield: 6 bottles

Imperial/metric	American
1 pint/0.6 litres elderflower blossoms	2½ cups elderflower blossoms
1 orange	1 orange
2 lemons	2 lemons
½ lb/225 g sultanas	½ lb golden raisins
1 gallon/4.5 litres boiling water	5 quarts boiling water
All-purpose wine yeast and nutrient	All-purpose wine yeast and nutrient
2¼ lb/1 kg white sugar	4½ cups white sugar
Campden tablets	Campden tablets

Sterilize all equipment as needed. Start your records.

Collect the elderflower heads (by severing them from the main stalks). As soon as you can, remove the blossoms from their tiny individual stems (you can use a clean comb or fork but agile fingers are more precise); it is important to ensure that no green stems are included with the blossoms since they often impart a rather unpleasant bitterness to the wine.

Place the blossoms in a measuring jug and shake them down gently; do not press. Pare the orange and lemons, avoiding all white pith. Chop the rind and set it aside. Express and strain the juice and set aside. Wash and chop the sultanas.

Put the blooms into a plastic bin with the orange and lemon rinds, and the sultanas. Pour over the boiling water and leave to cool. Stir in the orange and lemon juice, activated yeast and nutrient, cover loosely and leave to ferment for 5 days, pressing down on the floating flowers and fruit twice daily.

Strain the must through a nylon mesh bag into a container, pressing until all the juice is extracted. Stir in the sugar. Pour the liquid into a fermentation jar and any excess into a bottle. Fit an airlock into the fermentation jar and plug the neck of the bottle with cotton wool. Leave to ferment out at a temperature of about 68°F/20°C.

When fermentation is finished, move the wine to a cool place for a few days to help it to clear. Siphon the clearing wine off the sediment into a clean jar. Add 1 crushed Campden tablet and top up the jar (if necessary) with wine from the bottle. Bung tight, label and store in a cool place until bright and clear.

Rack again, then mature in bulk for 6 months before bottling. Keep for 1 year before drinking, and sweeten to taste before serving.

Cowslip Wine

This wine was once most highly regarded as a soporific. A glassful at bedtime was said to encourage a sound, natural sleep. Cowslips, however, are something of a rarity nowadays and the flower is protected by law. Packets of dried flowers can sometimes be bought in herbal shops, and although the resultant wine is naturally not quite as good as that made from fresh flowers, it does make an attractive wine.

Yield: 6 bottles

Imperial/metric	American
2 lemons	2 lemons
2 oz/50 g dried cowslip flowers	2 oz dried cowslip flowers
1 gallon/4.5 litres water	5 quarts water
1 lb/450 g white honey or 1 lb/450 g sultanas	1⅓ cups white honey or 1 lb golden raisins
1 lb/450 g white sugar	2 cups white sugar
All-purpose wine yeast and nutrient	All-purpose wine yeast and nutrient
Campden tablets	Campden tablets

Sterilize all equipment as needed. Start your records.

Thinly pare the lemons, avoiding all white pith, then chop the rind into small pieces. Express and strain the juice and set aside. Wash and chop the sultanas (raisins) if using them.

Put the dried flowers and the lemon rind into a plastic bin and pour on the boiling water. Stir in the honey (or add the sultanas (raisins), if you are using these instead), the sugar, then cover them and leave to cool. Add the activated yeast and nutrient and the lemon juice, cover loosely and ferment for 4 days, keeping the flowers submerged.

Strain out and press the flowers, and pour the must into a fermentation jar. Fit an airlock and continue the fermentation until finished. In due course, siphon the wine into a clean jar and add 1 crushed Campden tablet. Bung tight and label.

Keep for 3 months before bottling. Add 2 saccharin tablets per bottle before serving.

Variations: Other dried flowers may be used in a similar way, as can fresh primrose flowers. Although the aroma of primrose is not quite so charming as cowslip it still makes an attractive wine. Gather 1 gallon/4.5 litres (5 quarts) of primrose flowers and continue as described for *Cowslip wine*.

Frontiniac Wine

The following recipe is a modern adaptation of a traditional country wine.

Yield: 6 to 7 bottles

Imperial/metric	American
1 lb/450 g raisins	1 lb raisins
1 lemon	1 lemon
1 gallon/4.5 litres water	5 quarts water
2 lb/900 g white sugar	4 cups white sugar
½ pint/300 ml elderflower blossoms	1¼ cups elderflower blossoms
All-purpose wine yeast and nutrient	All-purpose wine yeast and nutrient
Campden tablets	Campden tablets

Sterilize all equipment as needed. Start your records.

Wash and chop the raisins. Express and strain the juice from the lemon. Place the raisins, water and sugar in a pan and simmer for 1 hour. Set aside to cool, then add the elderflower florets (see page 86 for how to pick and clean the florets). Cover and leave for 24 hours. Add the lemon juice and wine yeast and nutrient to the pan, cover and ferment on the pulp for 2 days.

Strain out and discard the pulp. Pour the must into a fermentation jar, fit an airlock to the jar and leave to ferment out in a warm place.

Siphon the clearing wine into a storage jar, bung tight, label and store for 3 months before bottling and using.

Rose Petal Wine

This delicious wine should be made from scented rose petals gathered from a number of different bushes. Gather the petals from full-blown roses at petal fall early on a dry sunny day. Rose petal wine makes a medium-sweet wine with a powerful aroma and flavour. Serve slightly chilled as a social wine.

Yield: 6 to 6½ bottles

Imperial/metric	American
½ gallon/2.25 litres rose petals	2½ quarts rose petals
1 orange	1 orange
2 lemons	2 lemons
½ lb/225 g sultanas	½ lb golden raisins
1 gallon/4.5 litres boiling water	5 quarts boiling water
All-purpose wine yeast and nutrient	All-purpose wine yeast and nutrient
2¼ lb/1 kg sugar	4½ cups sugar
Campden tablets	Campden tablets

Sterilize all equipment as needed. Start your records.

To measure the rose petals, put them into a measuring jug and shake them down gently; do not press. Pare the orange and lemons, avoiding all white pith, then chop the rind and set it aside. Express and strain the juice, wash and chop the sultanas (raisins).

Put the rose petals into a plastic bin with the orange and lemon rinds and the sultanas (raisins). Pour over the boiling water, cover and leave to cool. Add the fruit juice and yeast and nutrient, cover loosely and leave to ferment for 5 days, pressing down the floating petals and fruit twice daily. Continue as described for *Elderflower wine.*

Keep for 1 year before drinking, and sweeten to taste before serving.

Clary Wine

Clary is the blossom of the herb known as sage (Salvia officinalis). It makes a very strongly scented wine, most suitable for social drinking slightly chilled. Traditionally, it was considered to have aphrodisiacal qualities.

Yield: 6 to 6½ bottles

Imperial/metric	American
¾ pint/450 ml tender flowering clary tips	1 pint tender flowering clary tips
1 orange	1 orange
2 lemons	2 lemons
½ lb/225 g sultanas	½ lb golden raisins
1 gallon/4.5 litres boiling water	5 quarts boiling water
All-purpose wine yeast and nutrient	All-purpose wine yeast and nutrient
2¼ lb/1 kg white sugar	4½ cups white sugar
Campden tablets	Campden tablets

Sterilize all equipment as needed. Start your records.

Collect the flowering tips which cluster at the top of the plant (they are protected by pink and lavender bracts). Wash very gently and shake dry, then put them into a measuring jug and shake down gently; do not press.

Pare the orange and lemons, avoiding all white pith. Chop the rind and set it aside. Express and strain the juice, wash and chop the sultanas (raisins).

Put the flowering tips into a plastic bin with the orange and lemon rinds and the sultanas. Continue as described for *Dandelion wine.*

Scotch Broom or Gorse Wine

Mid-spring is regarded as the best time to gather these attractive golden flowers which can be found on open heathland, although they have a very long flowering season. There is an old country saying that, 'kissing is in season when the gorse is in bloom'—clearly intended to give plenty of scope to sweethearts! Broom or gorse wine was once regarded as a palliative for liver troubles and obesity, and Henry VIII of England is reputed to have drunk it regularly (to little effect, judging from his portraits). Gorse makes a fragrant, golden wine, best served cold as a social drink.

Yield: 6 bottles

Imperial/metric	American
1 gallon/4.5 litres gorse flowers	5 quarts gorse flowers
1 orange	1 orange
2 lemons	2 lemons
½ lb/225 g sultanas	½ lb golden raisins
1 gallon/4.5 litres boiling water	5 quarts boiling water
All-purpose wine yeast and nutrient	All-purpose wine yeast and nutrient
2¼ lb/1 kg sugar	4½ cups sugar
Campden tablets	Campden tablets

Sterilize all equipment as needed. Start your records.

To measure the gorse flowers, put them into a measuring jug and shake them down gently; do not press. Pare the orange and lemons, avoiding all white pith, then chop the rind and set it aside. Express and strain the juice, wash and chop the sultanas (raisins).

Continue as described for *Elderflower wine*.

Other Flower Wines

Other flowers can also be used to make wine—some of the better ones to use are as follows. Other ingredients and methods in each case are the same as for *Dandelion wine*.

Carnation wine

Use 4 pints/2.3 litres (5 pints) of the common garden 'pink' carnation. The clove carnation has too powerful an aroma.

Clover wine

Use 1 gallon/4.5 litres (5 quarts) of the purple clover blossoms.

Golden rod wine

Use only 1¼ pints/700 ml (3 cups) of the orange trumpets picked from the stalk. Take care not to include any stalk or green leaf.

Hawthorn blossom wine

Use 3½ pints/2 litres (2 quarts).

Lime bract and flower wine

Use 5 pints/2.8 litres (6¼ pints) of both bracts and flowers.

Pansy wine

Use 5 pints/2.8 litres (6¼ pints) of the large, velvety blooms as soon as they are fully open.

Herb and Leaf Wines

Although herbs and leaves do not seem, at first glance, to be particularly suitable ingredients for making wine, some splendid wines can be made from them. Traditionally, herbal wines were considered to have important therapeutic qualities and were frequently used as medicines. Their popularity suffered a decline in the nineteenth century during the movement of people from the countryside to the towns and cities, but they now seem to be enjoying a revival.

The varying pressures of modern society often cause depression, loneliness and psychosomatic ailments that do not respond to chemotherapy. Herbal therapy is sometimes more successful and certainly there can be no doubt that a well-made herbal wine can do you nothing but good. Whether this is due to the mystic qualities of the herbs, or the alcohol, or the company with which the wine is shared, is less certain!

Sadly, few of us today know how to recognize many of the herbs that grow in the hedgerows, so it is perhaps fortunate that many of them can be obtained from herbalists or larger supermarkets. A small 2-3 oz/50-75 g packet is usually sufficient to make six bottles of wine. Do not use the herb seeds offered in seedsman's catalogues to make wine—they are often treated with chemicals to help them germinate or to protect them from insects or bacteria.

Herbs need to be mixed with other ingredients, such as parsnips, carrots, beetroots (beets), malt extracts, flaked barley, flaked maize (cracked corn), flaked rice, flaked wheat or fresh or dried fruits to give the resultant wine some body.

Tree Leaf Wine

The young mature leaves of oak and walnut trees can be used to flavour wine. The recipe given below makes a pleasant wine, best served cold or slightly chilled.

Yield: 6 bottles

Imperial/metric
6 pints/3.35 litres oak leaves
  or 1 pint/550 ml walnut
  leaves
2 lemons
1 gallon/4.5 litres water
1 lb/450 g sultanas or raisins
All-purpose wine yeast and
  nutrient
2¼ lb/1 kg white sugar
Campden tablets

American
15 cups or 7½ pints oak
  leaves or 2½ cups walnut
  leaves
2 lemons
5 quarts water
1 lb golden raisins or raisins
All-purpose wine yeast and
  nutrient
4½ cups white sugar
Campden tablets

Sterilize all equipment as needed. Start your records.

Wash the young oak or walnut leaves in running water and shake them dry in a salad basket or colander. Chop them up lightly and put them into a measuring jug, shaking them down gently; do not press. Thinly pare the lemon rinds, avoiding all white pith. Express and strain the juice and set aside. Wash and chop the sultanas or raisins.

Continue as described for *Agrimony wine*. *Note:* These leaves contribute only tannin and a little flavour. It is essential to include the lemons to provide acid and the sultanas or raisins to provide some body and vinosity. An equal quantity of honey may be substituted for up to half the sugar, if desired.

Agrimony Wine

Agrimony makes a pleasant light 'tonic' wine, which should be served cool.

Yield: 6 bottles

Imperial/metric	American
1¾ pints/1 litre fresh agrimony leaves or 2 oz/50 g dried agrimony leaves	1 quart fresh agrimony leaves or 2 oz dried agrimony leaves
2 lemons	2 lemons
1 lb/450 g sultanas	1 lb golden raisins
1 gallon/4.5 litres water	5 quarts water
All-purpose wine yeast and nutrient	All-purpose wine yeast and nutrient
2¼ lb/1 kg white sugar	4½ cups white sugar
Campden tablets	Campden tablets

Sterilize all equipment as needed. Start your records.

Wash the leaves in running water, chop them up and put them into a boiling pan. Thinly pare the lemon rinds, avoiding all white pith. Express and strain the juice, wash and chop the sultanas (raisins).

Bring the water, agrimony leaves and lemon parings to the boil. Simmer for 10 minutes, then strain into a bin containing the sultanas (raisins). Discard the herbs and parings, top up with cold water and, when cool, add the lemon juice and the activated wine yeast and nutrient. Cover loosely and ferment for 5 days.

Strain out, press and discard the sultanas (raisins). Stir in the sugar. Pour the must into a fermentation jar and any excess into a bottle. Fit an airlock to the jar and a plug of cotton wool into the neck of the bottle. Ferment out at around 64°F/18°C.

Siphon the clearing wine into a clean jar, add 1 crushed Campden tablet, top up with wine from the bottle, bung tight and label.

Store for 3 months before bottling.

Mint Wine

Several varieties of mint are suitable for making wine, but the best results are obtained from garden mint, spearmint and peppermint. This recipe produces a light, slightly piquant wine, best served cool or slightly chilled.

Yield: 6 bottles

Imperial/metric	American
1¾ pints/1 litre fresh mint leaves	1 quart fresh mint leaves
2 lemons	2 lemons
1 lb/450 g sultanas	1 lb golden raisins
1 gallon/4.5 litres water	5 quarts water
All-purpose wine yeast and nutrient	All-purpose wine yeast and nutrient
2¼ lb/1 kg white sugar	4½ cups white sugar
Campden tablets	Campden tablets

Sterilize all equipment as needed. Start your records.

Wash the leaves in running water, chop them up and put them into a boiling pan. Thinly pare the lemon rinds, avoiding all white pith. Express and strain the juice, wash and chop the sultanas (raisins).

Continue as described for *Agrimony wine*.

Balm Wine

Balm leaves exude a subtle lemon aroma which comes through in this delicate white wine. The leaves of lemon thyme and lemon verbena can be used to make a similar wine.

Yield: 6 bottles

Imperial/metric
4 pints/2.25 litres fresh balm
   leaves
2 lemons
1 lb/450 g sultanas
1 gallon/4.5 litres water
All-purpose wine yeast and
   nutrient
2¼ lb/1 kg white sugar
Campden tablets

American
5 pints fresh balm leaves
2 lemons
1 lb golden raisins
5 quarts water
All-purpose wine yeast and
   nutrient
4½ cups white sugar
Campden tablets

Sterilize all equipment as needed. Start your records.

Wash the fresh leaves in running water, chop them up and put them into a boiling pan. Thinly pare the lemon rinds, avoiding all white pith. Express and strain the juice, wash and chop the sultanas.

Continue as described for *Agrimony wine*.

Mixed Herb Wine

Various herbs can be mixed together to make an unusual social wine. Any combination can be used but agrimony, comfrey, rosemary, thyme and balm are the most popular.

Yield: 6 bottles

Imperial/metric
1 lb/450 g parsley leaves
2 oz/50 g mint leaves
2 oz/50 g mixed other herbs
   (see above)
2 lemons
1 oz/25 g root ginger
1 lb/450 g sultanas
1 gallon/4.5 litres water
All-purpose wine yeast and
   nutrient
2¼ lb/1 kg white sugar
Campden tablets

American
1 lb parsley leaves
2 oz mint leaves
2 oz mixed other herbs (see
   above)
2 lemons
1 oz piece ginger root
1 lb golden raisins
5 quarts water
All-purpose wine yeast and
   nutrient
4½ cups white sugar
Campden tablets

Sterilize all equipment as needed. Start your records.

Remove the parsley and mint leaves from their stalks. Take care not to include any stalks with the leaves. Wash the parsley, mint and other herb leaves in running water, chop them up and put them into a boiling pan. Thinly pare the lemon rinds, avoiding all white pith. Express and strain the juice and set aside. Bruise the root ginger so that the flavour can exude into the liquid. Wash and chop the sultanas (raisins).

Bring the water, various herb leaves, lemon parings and bruised root ginger to the boil.

Continue as described for *Agrimony wine*.

NettleWine

Although this wine has been made for many centuries, the green colour is not very attractive and the wine has a slightly bitter taste, similar to that of hops. Even if it is not the most attractive-tasting wine, however, it is very rich in iron and vitamin C and is therefore still drunk—as it was traditionally—as a tonic. The common stinging nettle is the plant used and anyone who doesn't actively seek nettle stings should wear gloves while gathering them! Use only the tops and the young leaves.

Yield: 6 bottles

Imperial/metric	American
4 pints/2.25 litres young nettle tops	5 pints young nettle tops
2 lemons	2 lemons
½ oz/15 g root ginger	½ oz piece ginger root
1 lb/450 g sultanas	1 lb golden raisins
1 gallon/4.5 litres water	5 quarts water
All-purpose wine yeast and nutrient	All-purpose wine yeast and nutrient
2¼ lb/1 kg sugar	4½ cups white sugar
Campden tablets	Campden tablets

Sterilize all equipment as needed. Start your records.

Pick the tops and young leaves of the nettle plant, discarding any coarse stem or withered leaves. Wash them carefully in running water and put them into a boiling pan.

Thinly pare the lemon rinds, avoiding all white pith. Express and strain the juice and set aside. Firmly bruise the root ginger so that the flavour can exude into the liquid. Wash and chop the sultanas (raisins).

Bring the water, leaves, lemon parings and bruised root ginger to the boil. Simmer for 45 minutes, then strain into a bin containing the sultanas (raisins).

Continue as described for *Agrimony wine.*

TeaWine

If large quantities of tea are wasted in your household, then this is the wine for you! It makes a delicious social wine.

Yield: 6 bottles

Imperial/metric	American
1 gallon/4.5 litres strong cold tea	5 quarts cold strong tea
2 lemons	2 lemons
1 lb/450 g raisins	1 lb raisins
All-purpose wine yeast and nutrient	All-purpose wine yeast and nutrient
2¼ lb/1 kg sugar	4½ cups sugar
Campden tablets	Campden tablets

Sterilize all equipment as needed. Start your records.

Collect the tea left over from the pot after each brew until you have a gallon. Alternatively, pour a gallon (5 quarts) of boiling water on to 16 tea bags and leave covered until it is cool. Remove, press and discard the bags.

Thinly pare and chop the lemon rinds, avoiding all white pith. Express and strain the juice. Wash and chop the raisins.

Put the cold tea, the lemon rinds and juice, raisins and activated yeast and nutrient into a plastic bin. Ferment for 5 days, keeping the raisins submerged. Strain out, press and discard the raisins and rind. Stir in the sugar.

Pour the must into a fermentation jar and any excess into a bottle. Fit an airlock to the jar and a plug of cottonwool into the neck of the bottle. Ferment out and continue as described for *Agrimony wine.*

Folly Wine

The summer prunings of vines or blackberries are used for this wine. It makes a most attractive light white wine, best served chilled as an aperitif.

Yield: 6 bottles

Imperial/metric	American
6 lb/2.7 kg prunings	6 lb prunings
2 lemons	2 lemons
½ lb/225 g sultanas	½ lb golden raisins
1 gallon/4.5 litres water	5 quarts water
2¼ lb/1 kg sugar	4½ cups sugar
Campden tablets	Campden tablets
All-purpose wine yeast and nutrient	All-purpose wine yeast and nutrient

Sterilize all equipment as needed. Start your records.

Use only the young leaves and shoots cut off the vine after the fruit has set. Do not use them if they have recently been sprayed with copper sulphate or similar fungicide. Wash them in clean cold water and chop them up, discarding any tough pieces of stem. Thinly pare the lemons, avoiding all white pith. Express and strain the juice, wash and chop the sultanas (raisins).

Boil the prunings and lemon rinds in the water for 15 minutes. Strain into a bin, press and discard the pulp. Add the sultanas (raisins) and lemon juice and, when cool, the activated yeast and nutrient. Cover loosely and ferment for 5 days, keeping the fruit submerged. Strain out, press and discard the fruit.

Stir in the sugar and pour the must into a fermentation jar. Ferment out as described for *Agrimony wine*.

Variations: Bramble shoots are used in the same way, but wear leather gloves when handling them!

Parsley Wine

Parsley is probably the most popular of all the herb wines. The recipe given below makes a delightful, social wine—if you wish to convert it to a white table wine, reduce the quantity of sugar to 1¾ lb/770 g (3½ cups). Chilled white parsley table wine is a fragrant accompaniment to baked and other fish dishes, and also makes a piquant marinade for fish dishes.

Yield: 6 bottles

Imperial/metric	American
1 lb/450 g parsley leaves	1 lb parsley leaves
2 lemons	2 lemons
1 lb/450 g sultanas	1 lb golden raisins
1 gallon/4.5 litres water	5 quarts water
All-purpose wine yeast and nutrient	All-purpose wine yeast and nutrient
2¼ lb/1 kg white sugar	4½ cups white sugar
Campden tablets	Campden tablets

Sterilize all equipment as needed. Start your records.

Remove the parsley leaves from the main stalk. Take care not to include any stalks with the leaves. Wash the leaves in running water, chop them up and put them into a boiling pan. Thinly pare the lemon rinds, avoiding all white pith. Express and strain the juice, wash and chop the sultanas (raisins).

Continue as described for *Agrimony wine*.

Overleaf: Cold tea and nettles seem unlikely ingredients, but they can produce results quite as delicious as the ever-popular parsley wine.

Wines from Grains & Spices

Cereals contain very little fermentable sugar but a considerable amount of starch. Ordinary wine yeast is unable to ferment starch although a yeast called *Saccharomyces diastaticus* and marketed under the name 'cereal' yeast will ferment a small amount. The starch can also be converted to some extent by the inclusion in the must of a quantity of diastatic malt syrup, often just called DMS.

Cereal is lacking in acid, although it contains a good supply of nitrogen. It is necessary, then, to include acid either as lemon juice or citric acid crystals. Almost all traditional recipes included raisins to provide vinosity, leaving the cereal to provide just body and flavour.

The resultant wines often have a distinctive but not unpleasant cereal flavour. They can become very strong and make a good base for blending with thinner, more acid wines. They were probably originally made in those country areas where cereals were widely grown and where there was a lack of fruits, both from hedgerows and orchards. Some recipes included vegetables, especially potatoes. Cereal wines can take three years of maturation to reach their very best, but the results can be superb.

Although spices have long been available to the countryman only ginger has become established as a spice wine.

Maize Wine

Yield: 7 bottles

Imperial/metric
1½ lb/675 g flaked maize
4 sweet oranges
1 lemon
1 lb/450 g sultanas or raisins
1 gallon/4.5 litres boiling water
Cereal wine yeast and nutrient
3 lb/1.35 kg Demerara sugar
Campden tablets

American
1½ lb cracked corn
4 sweet oranges
1 lemon
1 lb golden raisins or raisins
5 quarts boiling water
Cereal wine yeast and nutrient
7 cups light brown sugar
Campden tablets

Sterilize all equipment as needed. Start your records.

Place the flaked maize (cracked corn) in a bin. Thinly pare the orange and lemon rinds, avoiding all white pith. Express and strain the juice. Wash and chop the sultanas (raisins).

Add the citrus rinds and sultanas (raisins) to the bin and pour over the boiling water. Stir well, cover and leave to cool. Add the activated cereal wine yeast and nutrient and the orange and lemon juice. Cover loosely and ferment on the pulp for 7 days, keeping the pulp submerged.

Strain out, press and discard the pulp. Stir in one-third of the sugar and continue as described for *Barley wine*.

Keep for 1 year before bottling and then for a further 6 months before tasting. It is wise to bottle in some half and some full bottles so that the half bottles can be tried first.

Barley Wine

This wine is not to be confused with the barley wine made from malt and hops. This wine is almost twice as strong, lighter in colour and takes years to mature. By then it is golden in colour, grainy in aroma, very strong, sweet and very smooth. It is dessert wine in the sense of one to drink after an evening meal. Crushed wheat can be substituted for the barley.

Yield: 7 bottles

Imperial/metric	American
1 lb/450 g old potatoes	1 lb old potatoes
2 lemons	2 lemons
1 lb/450 g raisins	1 lb raisins
1 lb/450 g crushed, flaked or pearl barley	1 lb crushed, flaked or pearl barley
1 gallon/4.5 litres boiling water	5 quarts boiling water
¼ lb/115 g diastatic malt syrup	¼ lb diastatic malt syrup
Cereal wine yeast and nutrient	Cereal wine yeast and nutrient
3 lb/1.35 kg Demerara sugar	7 cups light brown sugar
Tokay wine yeast and nutrient	Tokay wine yeast and nutrient
Campden tablets	Campden tablets

Sterilize all equipment as needed. Start your records.

Make this wine during the winter when main crop potatoes are old but not seeding. Scrub them thoroughly, cut them up into dice-sized pieces or thin slices. Thinly pare the lemons, avoiding all white pith, and express and strain the juice. Wash and chop the raisins.

Put the potatoes into a bin with the barley, lemon rind and raisins. Pour over the boiling water, cover and leave to cool. Meanwhile, dilute the malt syrup with an additional cupful of tepid water in a bowl, add the cereal yeast and beat in plenty of air. Leave until the barley must is cool.

Add the barley must mixture and lemon juice to the bin and stir well. Cover loosely and ferment on the pulp for 7 days, keeping the pulp submerged. Strain out, press and discard the pulp. Stir in one-third of the sugar. Pour the must into a fermentation jar and any excess into a bottle. Fit an airlock to the jar and plug the neck of the bottle with cotton wool. Ferment for 1 week.

Remove half the wine from the jar and stir in another third of the sugar. When it is completely dissolved, add the activated Tokay yeast and return the wine to the jar and any excess to the bottle. After a further week, again remove half the wine from the jar, stir in the last of the sugar and, when it is dissolved, return it to the jar and the excess to the bottle. Leave the wine until fermentation is finished, then siphon the clearing wine off the sediment into a clean jar. Top up from the bottle, add 1 crushed Campden tablet, bung tight, label and store the wine until it is bright.

The wine and sediment left in the jar may be poured into the bottle and left in a cool place until the sediment settles. The clear wine should then be transferred to another bottle and the sediment discarded. This wine can be used for topping up the jar after its racking.

Store in bulk for at least 2 years, then bottle and keep for a further year or more. It does not really begin to be enjoyable until it is at least 3 years old but by then it is very smooth indeed.

Rice Wine

Brown rice can be bought from certain supermarkets and most health food shops. It makes a strong social wine.

Yield: 6 bottles

Imperial/metric
3 lb/1.35 kg crushed brown rice
2 lemons
1 lb/450 g raisins
1 gallon/4.5 litres boiling water
Cereal wine yeast and nutrient
3 lb/1.35 kg white or light brown sugar
Campden tablets

American
3 lb crushed brown rice
2 lemons
1 lb raisins
5 quarts boiling water
Cereal wine yeast and nutrient
6 cups white or 7 cups light brown sugar
Campden tablets

Sterilize all equipment as needed. Start your records.

If the rice is not already crushed, grind it coarsely in a mincing machine. Alternatively, soak it in a little hot water for an hour to soften it a little. Drain off the surplus water, place the grains on a hard smooth surface and roll them with a ceramic or hard-wood roller to crack grains. (Polished rice is not so suitable. Flaked rice could be used, but much of the goodness has gone.)

Make the wine in the same way as described for *Barley wine.*

Variations: A quick maturing version of this wine is sometimes made with ordinary long-grain white rice instead of the brown rice. The sugar is reduced to 2¼ lb/1 kg (4½ cups white or 5¼ cups light brown) and is added in one dose after the raisins have been fermented and strained out. Other ingredients and methods are as already described. This wine is often ready for drinking when it is only 6 months old, but it does lack the distinctive character of brown rice wine.

Wheat Wine

Yield: 6 bottles

Imperial/metric
2 lb/900 g crushed wheat
2 lemons
2 sweet oranges
1 lb/450 g raisins
1 gallon/4.5 litres boiling water
Cereal wine yeast and nutrient
3 lb/1.35 kg Demerara sugar
Campden tablets

American
2 lb crushed wheat
2 lemons
2 sweet oranges
1 lb raisins
5 quarts boiling water
Cereal wine yeast and nutrient
7 cups light brown sugar
Campden tablets

Make the wine in the same way as described for *Barley wine.* Mature it for at least 1 year in bulk and 1 year in bottles before drinking.

Previous page: Rice, wheat and ginger, three distinctive cereal wines which are also suitable for blending with thinner, more acidic wines.

Ginger Wine

This wine is quite strong and should be used as a tonic. Serve as a warming welcome to guests on a cold night, or drink a glassful when you feel a cold coming on or have a sore throat. It is not suitable as a table wine, or for serving to children.

Yield: 6 bottles

Imperial/metric	American
3 oz/75 g root ginger	3 oz ginger root
3 lemons	3 lemons
1 lb/450 g raisins	1 lb raisins
¼ tsp/1.25 ml cayenne pepper	¼ tsp cayenne pepper
7 pints/4 litres boiling water	1 gallon plus 1½ cups boiling water
All-purpose wine yeast and nutrient	All-purpose wine yeast and nutrient
3 lb/1.35 kg Demerara sugar	7 cups light brown sugar
Campden tablets	Campden tablets

Sterilize all equipment as needed. Start your records.

Firmly bruise the ginger. Thinly pare the lemons, avoiding all white pith. Express and strain the lemon juice and set aside. Wash and chop the raisins. Put the ginger, lemon rind and raisins into a bin with the cayenne and pour on the boiling water. Stir the mixture thoroughly, then cover and leave to cool.

Add the activated wine yeast and nutrient and the lemon juice. Loosely cover the bin and ferment on the pulp for 7 days, keeping the pulp submerged. Strain out, press and discard the solids and then continue as described for *Barley wine*.

Store this wine in bulk for 6 months and then for a further 6 months in bottle. The wine may be coloured green with a few drops of food dye if you so wish.

Variations: Some of the sugar may be replaced with an equal quantity of honey. Three or four ripe bananas may be peeled, mashed and added to the sultanas or raisins to improve the body of the wine.

One fluid ounce/25 ml (2 tablespoons) of glycerine may be stirred in at the first racking to give the wine some extra smoothness. The cayenne may be replaced by a teaspoonful/5 ml of capsicum capsicum.

Half an ounce of citric acid/15 g may be used instead of the lemons, but some flavour is then lost. Half a fluid ounce/15 ml (1 tablespoon) of essence of ginger may be used instead of root ginger if necessary.

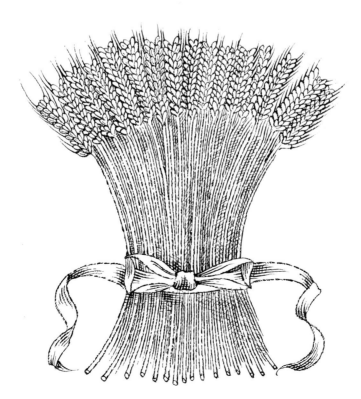

Tree Sap Wines

Due to the wide availability of other wines and ingredients, sap wines are no longer made very often. But they used to be very popular—Mrs Gaskell mentions birch wine in *Wives and Daughters* and the Russians were so partial to this wine that they decimated the birch trees around Hamburg from over-tapping during their occupation of that city in 1814. It is also reported that birch wine was a favourite drink of Queen Victoria and Prince Albert.

Birch trees of a suitable size are best tapped on a fine cold day in spring when the sap is running freely. The sap contains about 2 per cent sugar, but becomes infected when exposed to the air for more than twenty-four hours.

To tap a tree you need a drill, a length of thin rubber or plastic tube, a gallon jar, a piece of dowel rod the same diameter as the tube, some candle wax, and some cotton wool. In the early morning, drill a hole in the trunk about 20 in/50 cm from the ground. It should be from 1-1¼ in deep/2.5-3 cm and with a diameter of not more than ⁴/₁₀ in/1 cm. Into the hole push one end of the tube and ensure that it fits tightly. Do not push it in too far, otherwise the sap will not be able to enter the opening. Place the other end of the tube into a sterilized jar containing one crushed Campden tablet, and plug the neck around the tube with cotton wool.

Keep an eye on the flow of the sap. Sufficient may have been gathered in a few hours, or it may take a day or even two. Collect no more than 7 pints/4 litres (1 gallon plus 1½ cups), then withdraw the tube from the tree and plug the hole with the dowel rod. Push it well home and cover the end with candle wax.

For best results start to make the wine as soon as you reach home.

Birch Sap Wine

This wine is dry and may be served chilled as a white table wine.

Yield: 6 bottles

Imperial/metric	American
7 pints/4 litres fresh birch sap	1 gallon plus 1½ cups fresh birch sap
2 lemons	2 lemons
½ lb/225 g raisins	½ lb raisins
All-purpose wine yeast and nutrient	All-purpose wine yeast and nutrient
5 fl oz/150 ml cold tea (optional)	⅔ cup cold tea (optional)
2 lb/900 g white sugar	4 cups white sugar
Campden tablets	Campden tablets

Sterilize all equipment as needed. Start your records.

Thinly pare the lemons, avoiding all white pith. Express and strain the juice, wash and chop the raisins.

Simmer together the sap, lemon rinds and juice for 20 minutes, skimming off any scum that rises. Strain the hot liquid on to the raisins, cover and leave to cool. Add the activated yeast and nutrient, and if using, the cold tea. Ferment on the fruit for 5 days keeping the vessel loosely covered.

Strain out and press the raisins dry. Stir in the sugar. Pour the must into a sterilized fermentation jar and fit an airlock. Ferment out in a steady warm place. When fermentation is finished, move the jar to a cool place for a few days. Siphon the clearing wine into a sterilized storage jar, add 1 crushed Campden tablet, top up with cold boiled water and bung tight. Label and leave until bright then rack again.

Keep for 6 months before bottling.

Note: Saps lack acid and tannin and so the inclusion of some lemon juice is essential to a good fermentation and to a pleasant smell and taste. Half a cup of cold tea added to the must would improve its character still more.

Variations: If you would prefer a social wine for drinking between meals, the wine can be sweetened with 3 oz/75 g (6 tablespoons) of lactose at the bottling stage or, when serving, with caster (superfine) sugar or saccharin.

Sycamore tree sap and *Walnut tree sap* wines can be made in the same way.

Serving your Wines

Having taken great pains to produce excellent wines, it would be a pity to spoil them by not serving them to their best advantage. Most home winemakers serve their wines far too young. Anxious to taste them, they often drink them long before they are adequately mature. Some wines develop quickly and are at their best when still young and fresh, but most wines need a period of maturity in bulk and another in bottle. Wines that are light in alcohol, body and flavour usually develop most quickly and are often ready for drinking some three months after making them. This applies especially to some flower wines and to wines from canned fruits and canned fruit juices. Stronger wines with higher proportions of fruit ingredients, acids, tannin and alcohol, take anything from one to three years to mature.

If you find it impossible to resist the temptation to taste your wines early, then try bottling them in half-size bottles or at least in some half-size bottles and some full-size bottles. By opening the half-size bottles at monthly intervals (not more frequently), you will be able to monitor the progress of the wine and still have some full-size bottles left when the wine is mature and at its best. It will keep for several years, at least, so there is no great hurry to drink from fear of losing it.

It is a waste of a good mature wine to serve it for a purpose with which it is not compatible. Wines belong to certain categories: aperitif; table; dessert; sparkling; social; and when to serve them is usually determined by whether they are dry or sweet. Whatever the type, wine is nearly always at its best when served within the context of its category. For example, a very dry red wine will taste very much better with a roast or a meat casserole than with sweet apple pie and cream. It is not even attractive as an aperitif, let alone as a dessert wine after dinner, or as a social wine when having conversation with friends or watching television. Similarly a light, medium-sweet flower wine will taste very much better by itself than when served with meat or fish or cheese, because the food would overpower its delicate flavour. Select your wines for their suitability, then, as well as for their maturity. If you have nothing suitable, then serve some other beverage instead and save your wine for a more appropriate occasion.

Once you have made your choice, prepare the wine carefully. Sparkling wines, white table wines and rosé wines, all taste much better when served chilled. Conversely, red wines taste best at what is described as room temperature. But this temperature varies from room to room at different times of the year—around 68°F/20°C is thought to be the ideal. In very hot weather when the room temperature is above 75°F/24°C the wine may have to be cooled. In very cold weather, red wines may have to be warmed slightly and this is best done by leaving the bottle in a warm room for a day or two, so that it can acclimatize gradually. Red wines should *not* be placed in front of a fire, on a radiator or in hot water, since this flattens their flavour. White wines may be chilled in the refrigerator for two hours or placed in a bucket of iced water for a quarter of an hour. The right temperature makes a significant difference to the taste and flavour of a wine.

A wine bottle, even with a fancy label, never looks as attractive as a clear decanter. Wine is usually stored in green bottles to keep out the light, but this detracts enormously from the colour of the wine at table; in fact, frequently it cannot be discerned at all. This in itself is a good enough reason for serving your wine in a colourless glass decanter. A short while in a decanter also helps a young wine to develop and improve both its bouquet and flavour. A very young red wine may need as much as eight or ten hours, although most need only one or two. Even white and rosé wines benefit from a short while in a decanter.

The wine should also be served in suitable glasses. A wine glass should be colourless and undecorated in any way, and should have a stem firmly attached to a foot or base and supporting an incurved bowl. White, rosé and sparkling wines show up best in a tulip-shaped glass, while red wines look best in a more spherical shape. The incurving helps to hold in the bouquet and prevent it from escaping; V-shaped and even straight-sided glasses should, therefore, be avoided. Fill the glasses to between a half and two-thirds of their capacity, to leave room for the bouquet to develop on top of the wine. Glasses should always be washed in hot soapy water, thoroughly rinsed, drained and dried. Store them mouth up so that they do not pick up any taint from the surface on which they are stored.

Stained decanters are best filled with water to which a tablespoonful/15 ml of bleach has been added. Leave them overnight and then empty and rinse them four or five times until there is no trace of bleach left. Sand, gravel, chains and the like only roughen the inner surface and encourage future staining. If possible serve your wine on a silver salver (tray) and lay a white cloth on the table, since this shows up the clarity and colour of the wine to perfection. Avoid highly coloured or dull surfaces since these detract from its appearance.

Most wines taste best when served with appropriate food, although some taste best on their own. In general, dry red wines taste best with red meats such as beef, lamb and game; dry white wines taste best with white meats such as pork and with poultry and fish. Rosé wines make excellent companions for cold meats and pâtés; sweet white table wines are best with desserts. Most wines are enjoyable with cheeses.

Lightly flavoured wines with lightly flavoured food and more strongly flavoured wines with more strongly flavoured foods is a good rule of thumb. Use wine in cooking too—one glassful is usually enough. Marinade meat and fish in dry wines (red or white); add sweet wines to fresh fruits. Use white wine instead of water when stewing fruit. For cooking purposes it is sufficient to pour the ends of bottles into one bottle reserved exclusively for culinary use.

When drinking your wines, first inspect and admire their clarity and colour, ten inhale and think about the bouquet. Next take a mouthful of wine, chew it slowly and swallow it. Note the greeting, its freedom from 'off' flavours, the balance, the flavour and texture and, after a few moments, the aftertaste or farewell, that lingers on. Enjoy every moment. Make the most of your wine.

If you have never given much thought to this subject before now, you may well be wondering whether all this advice is really worthwhile. Well, it's your wine and you can serve it how you please. But experience will confirm that home-made wines benefit at least as much, if not more, than commercial wines from proper selection, preparation and serving within their context. For some reason, the vast majority of home winemakers think of their wines as being inferior to commercial wines.

It is true, of course, that we cannot make wines to equal the great vintages of France,

Germany, Spain or Portugal. But we can and do make wines of a standard comparable with those everyday wines drunk by the people of wine-producing countries. Indeed, we can often make much better wines. We can certainly take a lot more care of them in the making, and it seems a pity not to take a similar care in the serving. Treat your own wines with the same care that you would lavish on a bottle of expensive commercial wine. You will be impressed by the results.

The following chart will help you to analyse the quality of your wines, once you have set some kind of standard in your mind. This can be achieved by tasting a number of inexpensive commercial wines. They will give you some idea of what standards you can reach.

Country wines tend to have a strong aroma from the ingredients from which they were made, but there is no reason why they cannot compare well with wines made from grapes. The flavour will be different but not the quality.

By inspecting, smelling and tasting your wines objectively, you can become more conscious of their attributes. You will then be better able to improve them in another year by using more or less of a particular ingredient, or by adding something not previously included, for instance grape tannin.

Evaluating your wines critically enables you to differentiate between your best and your less good wines. You need not then suffer the embarrassment of offering an excellent wine to someone who does not appreciate wine and seeing them fidget with it, then leave most of it in the glass—wasted! Conversely, you will not offer an inferior wine to someone you would like to impress. After a bit of practice with the chart you will quickly be able to sort out the virtues of your wines.

Evaluation Chart

Sight
Clarity: Star bright, clear, dull, veiled, deposit
Colour (white): Colourless, greenish, pale yellow, straw, gold, amber
(rosé): Watery pink, pale pink, pretty pink, orange brown
(red): Black-red, deep red, ruby, light red, blue-red, brown-red
Overall: Excellent, very good, good, fair, poor

Smell
Aroma: Fruity, flowery, spicy, vinous, other
Bouquet: None, slight, clean, pleasant, full, rich
General: Yeasty, vinegarish, mouldy, infected, peardrops
Overall: Excellent, very good, good, fair, poor

Taste
Sweetness: Very sweet, sweet, medium sweet, medium dry, dry, very dry
Acidity: Sharp, pleasant, bland, medicinal
Tannin: Soft, firm, hard, astringent
Body: Thin, light, medium, full, heavy
Texture: Prickly, smooth, oily
Flavour: Delicate, pleasant, pronounced, off, foul
Farewell: None, short, adequate, lingering
Overall: Excellent, very good, good, fair, poor

112

Ales, Beers and Cider

Ales, beers and cider have been made – and drunk – by country men and women for centuries. The crafts may have evolved and changed since their official appearance in the eleventh century *Domesday Book*, but enthusiasm for producing and partaking has gone from strength to strength.

Initially, brewing could be a rather hit or miss affair: fermentation, for instance, was considered to be an Act of God and was much misunderstood, so that the quality of any finished beverage could – and did – fluctuate wildly. But what was lacking in science could be compensated for by intuition and flair – so that even the most modest products of the countryside could become delicious, thirst-quenching drinks – nettles, spruce, treacle – all were transformed. By the nineteenth century, things had improved even more, and beer in particular was so popular that it was being brewed commercially. There were 'strong beers' for serious drinking (preferably after work) and 'small beers' which were considered more suitable for breakfast-time indulgence or for the slaking of daytime thirst.

Today, the quality of ales, beers and cider can be monitored easily and successfully by even the most inexperienced craftsman. No one needs much in the way of fancy equipment – in fact, by far the most difficult requirement is patience: to prevent tasting the finished product too soon! The recipes and techniques which follow seek to blend these traditional ideas and ingredients with modern methods – thus enabling the beer and cider-maker to obtain the very best of both worlds.

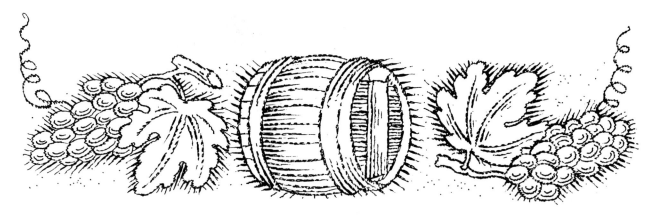

Ales and Beers

Ingredients

Water The serious country brewer has always been very conscious of the importance of his water supply. For many centuries it has been known that the springs and wells of different parts of the country were more suitable for some types of beer than others: the town of Burton-on-Trent in the English midlands, for instance, became famous for its bitter beers, flavoured by the mineral salts found in its many springs; Dublin, on the other hand, became known for stout, brewed with its soft water drawn up through the clay. In the United States, New York City brewers concentrate on beer, while in Newark, New Jersey the water is better suited to the brewing of ale.

The *quality* of the water is still very important in the brewing of good beer at home, but we now know how to treat the water we have wherever we live, so that we can make it suitable for whatever kind of beer we wish to brew. As a rule of thumb, if you live in a hard water area, then your water is most suitable for light ales and bitter beers, and if you wish to make brown ales, stouts or lagers, then you need to add a little salt to your water. The precise quantity to add depends on the hardness of your water and the quantity of beer being brewed, but as a rough guide, a quarter teaspoonful/1.25 ml of salt per Imperial gallon/4.5 litres (5 quarts) should be about right.

If you live in a soft water area, then this type of water enables you to brew splendid stouts and brown ales, but if you wish to make bitter beers then you must add hardening salts to your water. In the US these are called Burtonizing salts. They are usually available by the packet and are often made up locally by proprietors of home brew shops to suit the water of their locality. The salts consist of calcium sulphate, magnesium sulphate and calcium carbonate in slightly varying proportions. Again, the quantity to be added depends on the hardness of the water, but a rough guide would be half a teaspoonful/2.5 ml per gallon/4.5 litres. Some water boards include a fair measure of chlorine in the water to purify it. Since its flavour is far from attractive, drive it out by boiling the water vigorously for a few minutes before using.

Hops have been used in beer for many centuries but were first introduced into British beer in the fifteenth century. They were not at first popular. Gradually, however, their contribution to both flavour and preserving was recognized so that now they form the basic flavour in most commerical and home-made beers. In the past two decades or so, scientific research has produced new varieties of hop with better flavouring and preservative qualities which are now taking over from the familiar favourites of the past hundred or so years. At the time of writing, not all of the new varieties are as yet widely available so, in the meantime, old favourites such as *Goldings* can be mixed with a variety of

the more available new hops, such as *Wye Challenger*, to make superb beer. In the United States, *Yakima* hops predominate and it is difficult to find other varieties, but they do make an excellent brew.

Another new development is the hop pellet. Basically pellets are produced by grinding up the hops and compressing the powder; the hop essences and oils are therefore concentrated and so fewer pellets than loose hops are required to make beer. Depending on how the pellets are actually made, sometimes as little as half of the quantity of loose hops are needed, although more often it is nearer four-fifths.

Take great care when you buy hops or hop pellets. It is no longer enough just to ask for 'an ounce of hops'. You need to buy the right quantity and the right type: *Golding* for bitters and light ales, for instance, or a *Fuggle* for brown ales and stouts. In the US Fuggle hops are sold as *English Hop Extract*. Lagers, too, need their special hops, European varieties such as seedless *Styrian, Saaz* or *Hallertau* are best. Only *Hallertau* is currently available in the US.

Malt is the essence of beer. It provides fermentable sugar (maltose and dextrin) that can be turned into alcohol and also affects the colour, body and aroma of the finished drink. Most people nowadays will use an already prepared malt syrup or malt flour. There are different types available, each most suitable for a different type of beer—for instance, pale, which is best for light ales, medium, which is good for bitters and dark, which is good for stouts.

The real enthusiast, however, will probably want to prepare his own malt syrup direct from the grains of malted barley and to do this, he must purchase one of the varieties of malted barley available. The difference is in the roast: after the maltster has germinated the barley grains he roasts them to inhibit further growth—most grains are only lightly roasted so that the maximum amount of starch remains available for conversion into malt sugar. Lightly roasted grains are called pale malts and form the basis of every beer. Grains roasted for a little longer to give a slightly darker colour and stronger flavour are called crystal malts, and grains roasted for that much longer to produce an even darker colour and stronger flavour (although much less malt sugar) are

known as amber, brown or chocolate coloured malts. These latter malts are used for darkening brown ales and stouts. Finally, a black malt can be produced by roasting at a higher temperature, during which the starch is completely caramelized but not carbonated. The colour induces the domino black and that unique flavour so beloved in stout. Only small quantities of this are used in conjunction with other malts.

Additives Cereals are often added to homemade beers, both as a source of extra starch and to provide body, smoothness and improved 'head' to the resultant brew. They should be used sparingly. Torrified barley—grains heated until they look like popcorn—flaked maize (cracked corn or corn grits), flaked rice and wheat brewing flour are the most popular cereal additives, but raw barley is also sometimes used.

Sugar is normally added to beers to provide additional alcohol, although the coloured sugars can also provide some flavour. White granulated sugar is the most popular and effective sugar to add to beers, although light and dark brown sugars can also be used. Golden (light corn) syrup, black treacle (molasses), honey, glucose and invert sugar are all sometimes used in place of, or as well as, white

for the insertion of an airlock or an immersion heater coupled to a thermostat. They should also be translucent and graduated so that it is easy to fill them to the right level (in beermaking, you should always leave some headspace to allow for violent fermentation).

Masher/boiler If you intend to mash your grains you can buy an aluminium or stainless steel mashing vessel fitted with a strainer, a draw-off tap (faucet) and a heating element fitted with a thermostat. This will not only maintain the correct temperature for mashing the grains but can also be used for boiling the wort and the hops. Such special mashers are difficult to obtain in the US, but a large, heavy duty porcelain or stainless steel stock pot can serve the purpose very well. In this case, a kitchen thermometer and a large strainer will also be required.

granulated sugar. Never use more sugar than half the weight of the malt. Dried corn sugar prepared for brewing is available in US home brew shops.

Herbs and spices Although hops have been known and used for flavouring beer for 2000 years or more, they have only been universally used for the last 400 years. Before this time the basic flavour was provided by herbs—or the beer was left to be flavoured only by the malt. Among the most popular herbs for beer were nettles (the young leaves), yarrow, spruce and juniper berries. The most popular spice beer was ginger, still almost as popular today as it was in medieval Europe.

Bottles A selection of beer bottles with stoppers or crown caps in which to store the beer is also essential. Stoppers should have rubber rings in good condition and, if you are using crown caps, you will need a suitable tool for crimping them onto the bottles. It is unwise to use anything other than proper beer bottles, since others may not be strong enough to withstand the pressure of the gas in the beer (with explosive results!). A selection of different bottle sizes would be particularly useful.

Siphons are used in beermaking in the same way and for the same purpose as they are used in winemaking—to rack the beer off its sediment. You can either do as our forebears did and pour (or try to!) from the fermentation vessel into the bottles, without transferring sediment, or save clothing and sanity by sucking it up through a siphon. The different types of siphon available are discussed more fully on page 32.

Equipment

Fermentation bin A natural polythene (plastic) brewing bin with a lid is essential for fermenting beer. Our forebears used glazed earthenware vessels or wooden casks, but they are extremely heavy to handle and casks are also not easy to keep suitably clean. If you already possess a fermenting bin for use in winemaking, this would also be suitable for fermenting beer. If you are investing in a new one, then look for one fitted with a draw-off tap (faucet) and a lid with a removable grommet suitable

Miscellaneous items You will need a long-handled plastic or wooden spoon or paddle for stirring; a colander/strainer or nylon bag to strain the grains or hops; and a large boiling pan to boil the hops. All these items are hopefully part of your normal kitchen equipment, or can be adapted from items already in your everyday kitchen cupboard.

Some useful extras A polythene (plastic) funnel and a measuring jug have many uses. A kitchen thermometer will help to ensure that your grains are correctly mashed and that the yeast is never pitched at too high a temperature. A hydrometer will help to make your beers of the right strength.

Records, etc. As with wine, you should always keep a record of what quantity of each ingredient you put into your beer, and when you add it—then a particularly successful batch can be repeated, time and again. Any small notebook can be adapted to the task. Labels for your bottles can be bought from most home brew shops or you can fashion your own.

Yeast Beer cannot be brewed without yeast. As in wine, it reduces the sugars in the brewing mixture and turns them into alcohol. Brewer's yeast is the most suitable (at one time it could be bought from local breweries but alas there are fewer of them around now). Home brew shops sell both liquid and dried brewer's yeast in the varieties suitable for bitter beers, stouts and lagers. A single phial or sachet is enough for a brew, whether you are making one gallon or five/4.5 to 22.5 litres. Active dry yeast is sometimes used instead of brewer's yeast, especially in the United States.

Hygiene is as important in beermaking as it is in winemaking—and the principles and solutions necessary to sterilize equipment are the same. See, therefore, the section on Hygiene in part one (page 35).

Method

Mashing is the technical name for infusing malted barley grains and any cereal additives in hot water. During the process, the starch in the barley grains is converted by enzymes of the diastase group into maltose. It is the most crucial part of beermaking. The temperature of the water is important in mashing, and must be regulated between 140°F/60°C, for extraction of maltose and 158°F/70°C, for extraction of dextrin, an unfermentable sugar. Most brewers aim for a steady middle temperature of between 149°F/65°C and 152°F/66.5°C. In this way, they extract enough dextrin to give the beer some body, but also plenty of maltose for fermentation into alcohol. The grains need to be mashed in about two-thirds of the total quantity of water to be used. To make three Imperial gallons/13.5 litres (15 quarts) of beer, the grains should therefore be mashed in two gallons/9 litres (10 quarts) of water, appropriately adjusted for hardness and softness. The time taken to convert the starch to maltose will vary with the content of the mash and the consistency and degree of the temperature, but normally it will take a minimum of two hours, and it can take much longer.

End point: You can check to see whether all the starch has been converted into maltose and dextrin by using the iodine test. Place one tablespoonful/15 ml of the malt solution on a white saucer and add a few drops of ordinary household iodine. If the mixture turns blue or darkens in any way, starch is still present and the infusion must be continued for another half-hour before a further test is made, and until there is no colour change when iodine is added.

When mashing is complete, the malt solution must be strained out. Rinse the grains with a jugful of hot water (this is called 'sparging') to flush out the sticky maltose still adhering to the grains, which can then be discarded.

Boiling The hops and malt solution (the wort) must now be boiled together for up to an hour or so, to extract all the oils and essences from the hops, separate the protein from the wort and sterilize and stabilize it. A vigorous boil is required to agitate the hops sufficiently—a gentle simmer is not enough. Cover the pan to prevent excessive loss of flavour and vapour. At the end of the boil, turn the heat off but leave the pan where it is for a half-hour while the hops and protein settle on the bottom. Strain off into a fermentation bin or five gallon bottle and press the hops as dry as you can.

Topping up and adding yeast Add enough cold water to bring the total volume up to the required amount and to reduce the temperature. As soon as this is down to 65°F/18°C, add the yeast. The liquid yeast or dried granules can be sprinkled on direct, or they can first be re-activated—most experts recommend reactivating the yeast before adding, since it ensures a faster start to the fermentation and reduces the

Hops, the staple of British beer, in a traditional hop garden. New varieties are constantly becoming available to the home-brewer.

risk of infection from airborne bacteria. Add the granules or liquid to a diluted malt solution at least four to six hours before it is needed for the bulk fermentation. Half a pint per Imperial gallon/300 ml to 4.5 litres (5 quarts) is the ideal quantity of starter and the more that is required, the longer it should be left in a warm place (75°F/24°C). The air space above the solution should be of a similar volume to the solution itself, that is half a pint in a pint bottle (1¼ pint bottle), 300 ml in 550 ml, one pint in a quart bottle (2½ pint bottle), 550 ml in 1.2 litres, and so on. When the starter is fermenting vigorously, it should be pitched into the bulk of the wort.

Skimming and stirring The day after the yeast has been added, a thick frothy scum will appear on the surface of the fermenting wort. Skim off and discard since it will contain dirty specks of hop dust. The ring of yeast around the bin at surface level should also be removed with a clean cloth. Now stir up the wort to help the yeast absorb the oxygen it needs to reproduce itself and so replace the millions of cells removed in the scum. Re-cover the bin and leave in its even temperature.

Next day, repeat the skimming and stirring process then leave the brew to finish fermenting. By the fifth or sixth day you will see that all the bubbles have converged on the centre of the surface and then died away.

Clearing the beer Slowly sinking to the bottom of the bin will be millions more dead and living yeast cells and other debris from the fermentation. They must be removed to prevent them from spoiling the beer with the smell and taste of rotting vegetation. Move the bin to a cold place for a few days to encourage the settlement, or siphon into jars and fit with airlocks—the latter method leaves much of the paste behind in the bin and protects the beer from infection while clearing. It also stimulates the clearing. Finings may be added to hasten this process, but beers usually clear naturally if left for a few days.

Priming and bottling When the beer is fairly clear, siphon it into strong beer bottles, leaving an airspace at the top to allow for the gas pressure from the secondary fermentation. This is obtained from the priming sugar which must now be added. Ordinary white granulated, caster (superfine) sugar, glucose powder (dried corn sugar), or a sugar syrup can all be used. What is important is that the actual sugar content should not exceed half a level teaspoonful/2.5 ml per Imperial pint/550 ml (2½ cups).

Heat the water in the mashing boiler to 165°F/74°C, add the grain and flaked maize, and stir to prevent sticking. Lag the boiler and keep the temperature between 149° and 153°F/65° and 68°C, stirring every ½ hour or so.

Beer-making ingredients, including hops, sugar, flaked maize, malt grain finings and yeast. Assemble them together with the essential equipment: a thermometer, hydrometer, funnel and siphoning tube.

Less than this and the beer will lack life, vitality and good condition; more will produce a gassy beer with so much pressure that the residual yeast will lift up and cloud the beer when the bottle is opened.

When the priming sugar has been added, seal the bottle, label and leave in a warm room for a few days while the sugar is fermented. Then store the beer in a cool place for a few weeks to mature.

Draught beer Instead of siphoning the beer into bottles, it may be siphoned into a sterilized plastic pressure cask. These are available in two sizes, 10 and 25 litres (suitable for 2 and 5 gallon brews). Prime at the rate already indicated, seal the cask and leave in a suitable place. If you do not manage to drink all the beer before it loses vitality, the quantity remaining may be reprimed! Alternatively, a carbon dioxide (CO_2) injector can be fitted to the cask.

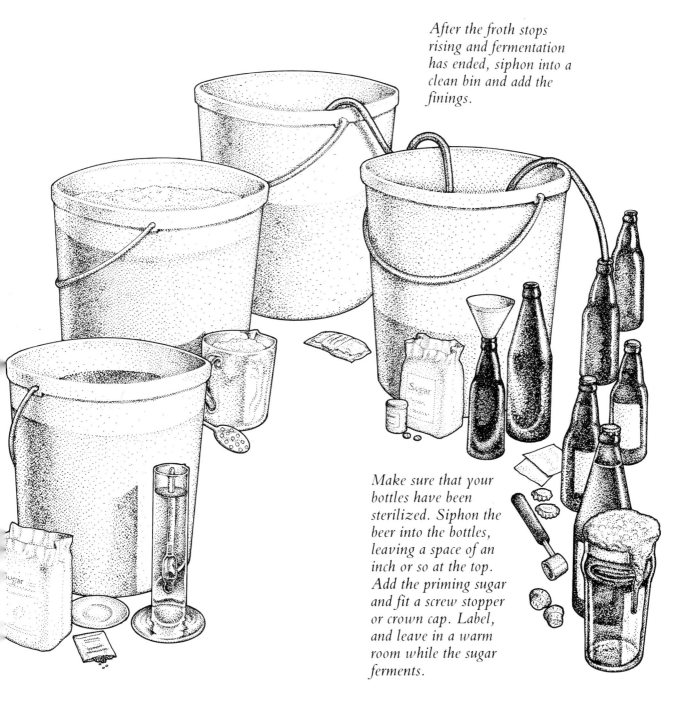

After the froth stops rising and fermentation has ended, siphon into a clean bin and add the finings.

Make sure that your bottles have been sterilized. Siphon the beer into the bottles, leaving a space of an inch or so at the top. Add the priming sugar and fit a screw stopper or crown cap. Label, and leave in a warm room while the sugar ferments.

Bitter

The classic British beer!

Yield: 16 pints/9 litres (10 quarts)

Imperial/metric	American
2 lb/900 g pale malt grains	2 lb pale malt grain
½ lb/225 g crushed crystal malt grains	½ lb light malt grain, crushed
¼ lb/115 g flaked maize	¼ lb cracked corn or corn grits
2 gallons/9 litres hard water	10 quarts hard water
1½ oz/40 g Wye Challenger hops or 2 oz/50 g Kent Goldings	1 oz Yakima hops
1 lb/450 g glucose powder	1 lb dried corn sugar
1 sachet beer yeast	3.5 g (½ packet) lager bottom yeast
8 tsp/40 ml caster sugar	8 tsp superfine sugar

Assemble the ingredients. Sterilize all equipment as needed. Start your records.

Heat 10 pints/5.6 litres (12½ pints) of water to a temperature of 158°F/70°C. Sprinkle the pale and crystal (light) malts, and the maize (cracked corn) on to the water, stir well and maintain a temperature of 151°F/66°C until the end point is reached—in about 2 hours or so.

Strain off the malt liquor through a strainer or nylon bag into a boiling pan. Spray the grains with 1 pint/550 ml (1¼ pints) of hot water and let this drain into the rest of the wort. Add all but a handful of the hops, wetting them thoroughly, bring to the boil and boil them vigorously, covered, for 45 minutes.

Leave for 30 minutes, for the hops to settle, then strain them out through the same strainer or bag. Spray them with 1 pint/550 ml (1¼ pints) of tepid water and drain all this into a fermentation bin. Discard the hops.

Stir in the glucose powder (corn sugar), top up with cold water to 2 gallons/9 litres (10 quarts) and, when the temperature is 64°F/18°C, add an activated yeast. Loosely cover the bin.

Next day, skim off the froth and stir up the beer. Repeat the process on the following day and afterwards add the remainder of the hops, wetting them thoroughly. Replace the cover and leave to ferment out (about 6 or 7 days), when the surface of the beer should be clear. Siphon the beer into sterilized fermentation jars and fit air locks. Discard the pasty sediment.

As soon as the beer looks fairly clear in a few more days, siphon it into 16 1-pint beer bottles and add ½ teaspoonful/2.5 ml of caster (superfine) sugar to each bottle. Screw in sterilized stoppers fitted with good rubber rings or securely crimp on crown caps. Label the bottles and leave them in a warm room for a few days while the sugar is fermented.

Store the beer in a cool place for 3 or 4 weeks before drinking.

Note: To serve the beer, carefully pour the beer down the inside of a suitable glass, without inverting the bottle which would cause a stirring up of the sediment.

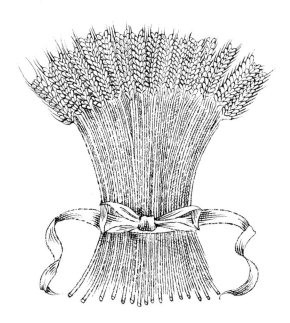

Draught Mild Ale

Yield: 16 pints/9 litres (10 quarts)

Imperial/metric
2 gallons/9 litres medium
   hard water
2 lb/900 g plain malt extract
1 oz/25 g Golding hops
1 sachet ale yeast
8 tsp/40 ml caster sugar

American
10 quarts medium hard water
2 lb dried malt extract
1 oz Yakima hops
3.5 g (½ packet) ale top
   yeast
8 tsp superfine sugar

Assemble the ingredients. Sterilize all equipment as needed. Start your records.

Warm half the water and dissolve the malt extract in it. Meanwhile, boil the hops in the other half of the water for 30 minutes. Strain the hop water into the malt solution, cover and leave to cool. Discard the hops. Add the yeast and ferment, skim and stir as described for *Bitter beer*.

When fermentation has finished, siphon the beer into a 2-gallon or 10-litre pressure keg. Stir in 8 level teaspoonfuls/40 ml of caster (superfine) sugar and seal the keg.

Store the beer in a cool dark place for 10 days before drinking.

Brown Ale

Yield: 16 pints/9 litres (10 quarts)

Imperial/metric
1¾ lb/550 g crushed pale
   malt grains
¾ lb/350 g crushed crystal
   malt grains
2 oz/50 g black malt grains
2 gallons/9 litres soft water
1 oz/25 g Wye Northdown
   or 1¼ oz/30 g Fuggle
   hops
1 sachet beer yeast
½ lb/225 g soft brown sugar

American
1¾ lb pale malt grain,
   crushed
¾ lb light malt grain,
   crushed
2 oz black malt grain
10 quarts soft water
3¾ tsp English hop extract
3.5 g (½ packet) ale hop
   yeast
1¼ cups soft brown sugar

Assemble the ingredients. Sterilize all equipment as needed. Start your records.

Follow the method as described for *Bitter beer*, but mash at the lower temperature of 145°F/63°C.

Variations: The above recipe is for a fairly dry brown ale. If you prefer a sweet one, add 6 oz/175 g lactose just before bottling.

Strong Ale or Barley Wine

This beer is fairly strong (around 9 per cent alcohol) and should therefore be treated with respect!

Yield: 8 pints/4.5 litres (5 quarts)

Imperial/metric
2 lb/900 g crushed pale malt
  grains
1 lb/450 g crushed crystal
  malt grains
¼ lb/115 g flaked rice
¼ lb/115 g flaked wheat
1 gallon/4.5 litres hard
  water
1 oz/25 g Challenger hops
1 sachet beer yeast
½ lb/225 g Demerara sugar
1 sachet Champagne wine
  yeast and nutrient

American
2 lb pale malt grain, crushed
1 lb light malt grain, crushed
¼ lb flaked rice
¼ lb flaked wheat
5 quarts hard water
1 oz Yakima hops
3.5 g (½ packet) ale top
  yeast
1⅓ cups brown sugar
1 sachet Champagne wine
  yeast and nutrient

Assemble the ingredients. Sterilize all equipment as needed (remember you will need a fermentation jar). Start your records.

Mash the grains, rice and wheat at a temperature of 153°F/67°C. Strain out the solution and rinse the grains with a jugful of hot water. Now add the hops and boil together for 45 minutes. Leave the liquor aside until the hops settle (about 30 minutes) then strain, press and discard the hops. Top up with cold water and, when cool, add the beer yeast.

Ferment, skim and stir as described for *Bitter beer,* but after the second skimming siphon the wort into a fermentation jar. Stir in the sugar and the activated Champagne wine yeast and nutrient. Fit an airlock and leave to ferment out.

Siphon into sterilized bottles, prime, seal and label.

Store for 1 year in a cool dark place before drinking.

Spruce Beer

This beer has a clean, fresh flavour and was traditionally regarded as spring medicine, especially in Scotland. There the young green shoots of the spruce tree were gathered and boiled to produce the flavouring. Nowadays, spruce extract can be bought from pharmacies or home brew shops.

Yield: 8 pints/4.5 litres (5 quarts)

Imperial/metric
1 lemon
1 lb/450 g Demerara sugar
1 tsp/5 ml spruce extract
1 gallon/4.5 litres water
1 tsp/5 ml granulated yeast
4 tsp/20 ml caster sugar

American
1 lemon
2⅓ cups light brown sugar
1 tsp spruce essence
5 quarts water
1 tsp active dry baker's yeast
4 tsp superfine sugar

Sterilize all equipment as needed. Assemble the ingredients. Thinly pare the lemons, avoiding all white pith. Express and strain the juice and set aside.

Place the sugar, lemon rind, lemon juice and spruce extract in a suitable container. Pour on the water just warm enough to dissolve the sugar and stir well. Cover the vessel and, when the wort is cool enough, add the yeast and ferment as for *Ginger beer.* When fermentation is quite finished, siphon into sterilized bottles and prime with the caster (superfine) sugar. Seal and label the bottle.

Store for 1 week in a cool dark place before drinking.

Dry Stout

This dark strong beer has a unique flavour.

Yield: 16 pints/9 litres (10 quarts)

Imperial/metric
2 gallons/9 litres soft water
1½ lb/675 g crushed pale
   malt grains
1 lb/450 g crushed crystal
   malt grains
¼ lb/115 g black malt grains
¼ lb/115 g flaked oats
1½ oz/40 g Wye Northdown
   or 2 oz/50 g Fuggle hops
1 lb/450 g dark brown sugar
1 sachet stout yeast

American
10 quarts soft water
1½ lb pale malt grain,
   crushed
1 lb light malt grain, crushed
¼ lb black malt grain
¼ lb flaked oats
4 tsp English hop extract
2⅓ cups dark brown sugar
3.5 g (½ packet) ale top
   yeast

Assemble the ingredients. Sterilize all equipment as needed. Start your records.

Follow the method as described for *Bitter beer* but mash at the lower temperature of 148°F/64.5°C.

Store in a cool dark place for about 6 weeks before drinking.

Sweet Stout

A sweeter version of the classic stout recipe given above.

Yield: 16 pints/9 litres (10 quarts)

Imperial/metric
2 gallons/9 litres soft water
1½ lb/675 g crushed pale
   malt grains
½ lb/225 g crushed crystal
   malt grains
¼ lb/115 g black malt grains
1¼ oz/30 g Wye
   Northdown or
   1¾ oz/45 g Fuggle hops
¾ lb/350 g dark brown sugar
1 sachet stout yeast
½ lb/225 g lactose

American
10 quarts soft water
1½ lb pale malt grain,
   crushed
1 lb light malt grain, crushed
¼ lb black malt grain
4 tsp English hop extract
2⅓ cups dark brown sugar
3.5 g (½ packet) ale top
   yeast
½ lb lactose

Assemble the ingredients. Sterilize all equipment as needed. Start your records.

Follow the method as described for *Bitter beer*, but mash at the lower temperature of 145°F/63°C. Just before bottling, sweeten with the lactose.

Store for 4 weeks before drinking.

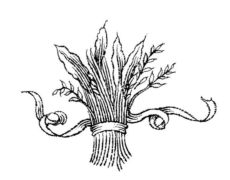

Cock Ale

This unusual recipe looks somewhat alarming at first reading but was once a great favourite with farmers and their workers. Originally an old cockerel would be killed, plucked, cleaned and flayed, that is, hit against a wooden table top until all the bones were crushed. It would then be added to a barrel of beer in the making. An adapted recipe for a smaller quantity is given below. It produces a splendid beer of great character.

Yield: 8 pints/4.5 litres (5 quarts)

Imperial/metric	American
Chicken bones, wings etc.	*Roasted chicken wings, bones etc.*
½ pint/300 ml dry white wine	*1¼ cups dry white wine*
1 lb/450 g malt extract	*1 lb dried malt extract*
½ lb/225 g golden syrup	*¾ cup light honey*
1 gallon/4.5 litres hard water	*5 quarts hard water*
¾ oz/20 g Golding hops	*½ oz Yakima hops*
1 sachet ale yeast	*3.5 g (½ packet) ale top yeast*
4 tsp caster sugar	*4 tsp superfine sugar*

Sterilize all equipment as needed. Start your records.

Break up the carcass, bones, wing tips, tail, neck, etc., of a plainly roasted chicken (no herbs), the flesh of which has already been carved and eaten. Include all the fragments left over from the carving. Place the chicken in a bowl or jug and pour over the dry white wine. Cover the vessel and leave in a cool dark place.

Dissolve the malt extract and syrup (honey) in a quarter of the water and boil the hops in the rest for 45 minutes. Strain the hop liquor into the malt and syrup (honey) solution and, when cool, add the yeast.

Next day, after the first scum has been skimmed from the beer, strain the wine from the chicken into the beer. Place the chicken bones, etc., in a muslin or nylon bag and suspend it in the fermenting beer for 3 days. Remove and drain the bag, stir the beer and leave it, loosely covered, in a warm place for the fermentation to finish.

Siphon the clearing beer into strong beer bottles, prime with ½ teaspoonful/2.5 ml of caster (superfine) sugar per pint/550 ml (1¼ pints), then seal and label.

Store for at least 3 weeks in a cool dark place before drinking.

Nettle Beer

Long before hops were added, ale was flavoured with various plants and herbs. Nettles were particularly popular. Use only the young tops of the plants and gather them before the plants flower as, after flowering, the chemical constitution of the nettle changes and it becomes mildly poisonous.

Yield: 8 pints/4.5 litres (5 quarts)

Imperial/metric	American
2 lb/900 g young nettle tops, leaves and stalks	2 lb young nettle tops, leaves and stalks
1 gallon/4.5 litres medium soft/hard water	5 quarts medium soft/hard water
1 lb/450 g plain malt extract	1 lb dried malt extract
1 sachet ale yeast	3.5 g (½ packet) ale top yeast
4 tsp/20 ml caster sugar	4 tsp superfine sugar

Gather the young nettle tops before the plant flowers (a good thick pair of gloves will be useful!). Wash the nettles and shake them dry. Assemble the other ingredients. Sterilize all equipment as needed. Start your records.

Warm a quarter of the water and dissolve the malt extract in it. Meanwhile, boil the nettles in the rest of the water for 15 minutes. Strain the nettle water into the malt solution, cover and leave to cool. Discard the nettles. When the liquor is cool enough, add the yeast.

Ferment, skim and stir as described for *Bitter beer*, and when fermentation has finished, siphon into sterilized beer bottles. Prime with the caster (superfine) sugar, seal and label the bottles.

Store for 1 week in a cool dark place before drinking.

Ginger Beer

Well chilled, this beer makes a very refreshing drink on a hot summer day. As it is only marginally alcoholic, it is also suitable for a children's party.

Yield: 8 pints/4.5 litres (5 quarts)

Imperial/metric	American
2 oz/50 g root ginger	2 oz ginger root
2 large lemons	2 large lemons
1 gallon/4.5 litres water	5 quarts water
¼ oz/15 g cream of tartar	2 tbsp cream of tartar
1 lb/450 g white sugar	2 cups white sugar
1 tsp/5 ml granulated yeast	1 tsp active dry yeast

Sterilize all equipment as needed. Bruise the ginger. Thinly pare the lemons, avoiding all white pith. Express and strain the juice and set aside. Bring the water to the boil.

Place the bruised root ginger, the cream of tartar, lemon rind and sugar in a suitable container, pour over the boiling water and stir well until the sugar is dissolved. When cool, add the lemon juice and yeast. Loosely cover with a sheet of polythene (plastic) tied down with wool and leave for 36 hours in a warm room. Skim off the frothy scum, siphon the ginger beer into STRONG bottles creating as little froth as possible. Seal tightly and store for 3 days in a cool place.

The beer is now ready for drinking.

Note: If ginger beer made by this method is kept for more than a few days, pressure may build up in the bottles. When opened there will be a tremendous gush of foam and the beer will be lost. The pressure may even be enough to burst a weak or thin bottle.

Variations: If you wish to make a ginger beer that will keep for some weeks, follow the above method but allow the fermentation to continue for 5 days and sweeten it with 2 or 3 saccharin tablets per bottle. More sugar will be fermented into alcohol and so it is not so suitable as a drink for young children. This version may be kept in a cool place for some weeks if necessary without causing undue pressure in the bottle. It may be mixed with bitter beer to make shandy.

Treacle Ale

This traditional recipe comes from Scotland where—according to tradition—it was sometimes used in porridge-making when milk was scarce or too expensive! The black treacle (molasses) gives the finished beer a very strong, slightly bitter flavour.

Yield: 8 pints/4.5 litres (5 quarts)

Imperial/metric	American
1 lemon	*1 lemon*
½ lb/225 g black treacle	*¾ cup molasses*
1 lb/450 g golden syrup	*1½ cups light honey*
1 gallon/4.5 litres warm water	*5 quarts warm water*
1 tsp/5 ml granulated yeast	*1 tsp active dry baker's yeast*

Sterilize all equipment as needed. Pare the lemon avoiding all white pith. Express and strain the juice.

Dissolve the treacle (molasses) and syrup in the water. Add the lemon rind, cover and leave to cool. Stir in the lemon juice and the yeast and ferment as described for *Ginger beer*. When fermentation is quite finished, siphon into sterilized bottles, seal and label. It is not necessary to prime this ale.

Store for 1 week in a cool dark place before drinking.

Honey Beer

This traditional recipe produces a beer with a quite pronounced honey flavour.

Yield: 8 pints/4.5 litres (5 quarts)

Imperial/metric	American
1 lemon	*1 lemon*
1½ lb/675 g dark honey	*2¼ cups dark honey*
1 gallon/4.5 litres water	*5 quarts water*
½ oz/15 g hops	*½ oz Yakima hops*
1 tsp/5 ml granulated yeast	*1 tsp active dry baker's yeast*

Sterilize all equipment as needed. Thinly pare the lemon, avoiding all white pith. Express and strain the lemon juice and set aside.

Dissolve the honey in a quarter of the water. Boil the hops and lemon rind in the rest of the water for 30 minutes. Strain the hop water into the honey solution and leave to cool. Discard the hops.

Add the yeast and the lemon juice. Leave to ferment in a warm place for 3 to 4 days and, when fermentation has finished, siphon into strong bottles. Prime in the usual way, seal and label the bottles.

Store for at least 2 weeks (preferably longer) in a cool dark place before drinking.

Variations: If you would prefer a less pronounced honey flavour, follow the above recipe but use 1 lb/450 g of malt extract and only ½ lb/225 g (1 cup) of dark honey.

Beetroot (Beet) Beer

Yield: 8 pints/4.5 litres (5 quarts)

Imperial/metric	American
2 lb/900 g new beetroots	2 lb new beets
½ oz/15 g root ginger	½ oz root ginger
1 gallon/4.5 litres water	5 quarts water
1 oz/25 g hops	½ oz Yakima hops
½ lb/225 g malt extract	½ lb dried malt extract
1 lb/450 g brown sugar	2⅓ cups brown sugar
1 sachet ale yeast	3.5 g (½ packet) lager bottom yeast

Trim, scrub and dice the beetroots (beets). Bruise the ginger. Sterilize all equipment as needed.

Boil the beetroots (beets) in the water with the hops for 1 hour. Stir in the malt extract, sugar and ginger and boil again for a further 15 minutes. Strain out the beetroot (beets), hops and ginger and discard. Cover the liquor and leave to cool.

Add the yeast and ferment for 1 week, keeping the bin loosely covered and skimming as necessary. When fermentation has finished, siphon into beer bottles and prime in the usual way. Seal and label the bottles.

Store the beer for 2 weeks in a cool dark place before drinking.

Cherry Ale

This is a very strong, still beer, with a rich cherry flavour.

Yield: 3 pints plus/almost 2 litres (about 2 quarts)

Imperial/metric	American
1 lb/450 g Morello cherries	1 lb sour cherries
1 lb/450 g white sugar	2 cups white sugar
3 pints/1.7 litres strong home-brewed ale (not barley wine)	2 quarts home-brewed ale (not barley wine)
1 sachet ale yeast	3.5 g (½ packet) ale top yeast

Sterilize all equipment as necessary. Start your records. Wash and stalk the cherries. Prick them all over with a sharp fork and place them in a container such as a large sweet jar.

Dissolve the sugar in the ale and pour over the cherries. Add the yeast, cover loosely and leave in a warm place until fermentation is finished. Move the beer to a cool place while the sediment settles, then siphon it into sterilized bottles, seal and label.

Store for 3 months in a cool dark place before drinking.

Variations: Other fruits may be used—for instance, ¼ lb/115 g of dried apricots or 1 lb/450 g of gooseberries cut up in a light ale, and 1 lb/450 g blackberries or damsons in a strong brown ale.

Cider

The best cider is made from varieties of apples particularly grown for the purpose. A blend of bitter sweet, bitter sharp and sweet sharp apples is best, the proportions varying with the quality of the fruit and the type of cider being made. The majority of the apples must be sweet in order to provide the sugar to make the alcohol but some acid, for freshness, and some bitterness, for character, are also essential.

The old varieties of apples which our forebears would have used for cidermaking have now almost died out and new dwarf ones that can be mechanically harvested are taking their place. For those without access to cider apples, however, a pleasant cider can be made from dessert, cooking and crab apples, providing the principle of blending is kept in mind. Cox's Orange pippins or other 'sweet' dessert apples make an excellent base for the sweet side, Bramleys or other cooking varieties for the sharp and John Downie, Siberia or other crab apples for the bitter.

A rule of thumb proportion is: 6 measures of sweet to 2½ sharp and 1½ bitter, but the proportion is not critical and 7/2/1 or 6/2/2 would also be satisfactory. Some 20 lb/9 kg of fruit is usually needed to produce an Imperial gallon/4.5 litres (5 quarts) of juice but this figure varies from season to season, with the ripeness and type of the fruit, and with the method of juice extraction used.

Once you have assembled the fruit, lay it out on trays for some weeks to mellow. Try to ensure that the apples are not touching one another—if one apple starts to go bad, the infection will not then spread to all the others. A cool dark place is best for storage, but if the apples must be stored in a light room, cover them with brown paper. Polythene (plastic) is not so suitable as it attracts condensation.

Once the fruit has mellowed, it must be washed thoroughly to remove all traces of leaf, grass, dust, and so on. Two crushed Campden tablets and half a teaspoonful/2.5 ml of citric acid dissolved in an Imperial gallon/4.5 litres (5 quarts) of cold water for the final rinse will also kill off any unwanted microbes! The fruit must now be crushed quickly and pressed. Speed is of the essence, since the besetting danger of cidermaking is oxidation. A cut apple left exposed to the air until it turns brown will have a flat taste, and this disappointing flavour can easily spoil home-made cider. A stainless steel blade attached to a stainless steel shaft that fits into the chuck of an electric drill makes an excellent and speedy crusher (see page 35). The bag used for straining and pressing the fruit should be sterilized with a sulphite solution, and a crushed Campden tablet for every Imperial gallon/4.5 litres (5 quarts) of juice in the receiving bin will also help to prevent oxidation.

Cider

This basic recipe is for a dry, still cider.

Yield: 8 pints/4.5 litres (5 quarts)

Imperial/metric	American
12-14 lb/5.5-6.5 kg eating apples	12-14 lb eating apples
4-5 lb/1.8-2.3 kg cooking apples	4-5 lb cooking apples
2-4 lb/900 g 1.8 kg crab apples	2-4 lb crab apples
½ tsp/2.5 ml citric acid	½ tsp citric acid
Campden tablets	Campden tablets
1 tsp/5 ml pectic enzyme	1 tsp pectic enzyme
Sugar	Sugar
Champagne wine yeast and nutrient	Champagne wine yeast and nutrient

Sterilize all equipment as needed. Start your records. Wash the fruit carefully, using 2 crushed Campden tablets and the citric acid dissolved in a gallon of cold water for the final rinse.

Crush the fruit as quickly and thoroughly as you can and place it at once in a sterilized nylon or hessian bag. Put the pectic enzyme and a crushed Campden tablet in the receiving bin (which should be just big enough to take all the juice) and press out the juice as hard as you can. Turn the fruit over in the bag several times and continue the pressing until the apple 'cake' is firm and dry.

When the pressing is complete, leave the apple juice sealed in the container for 24 hours.

Next day, activate a Champagne wine yeast and nutrient in a starter bottle. (Use a 20 fl oz/550 ml bottle and 10 fl oz/300 ml of liquid, i.e. 5 fl oz/150 ml apple juice and 5 fl oz/150 ml tepid water.) It will take about 6 hours for the yeast to become active, so in the meantime check the specific gravity of the apple juice. A hydrometer reading between 1.044 and 1.072 is desired. If the gravity is too low, stir in a little white sugar to raise it a few units.

Add the yeast, fit an airlock and leave to ferment in a cool place. A slow fermentation spread over 6 weeks produces a better flavour than one completed in 7 to 10 days, so aim for a fairly cool, even temperature (around 59°F or 15°C).

When fermentation has finished, leave the cider for a few days, then siphon it from its sediment of fruit pulp and yeast. If you are in a hurry, 1-2 tablespoonfuls/15-30 ml of fresh milk and 1 crushed Campden tablet may be stirred in to hasten the clearing. If the cider is already fairly clear, leave out the milk. As soon as the cider is bright, siphon it into sterilized, screw-stoppered bottles and label.

Store upright in a cool place for 4 to 6 months before drinking.

Variations: To produce a *slight sparkle* in the cider, prime the bottles with a ¼ teaspoonful/1.25 ml of caster (superfine) sugar per 20 fl oz/550 ml (2½ cups): no more!

A fully sparkling cider can be made in the same way as sparkling wine. When the cider is bright and 3 months old, siphon it into a fermentation jar. Stir in 2½ oz/70 g (⅓ cup) of caster (superfine) sugar and add an activated Champagne wine yeast. Fit an airlock and, as soon as the cider is fermenting, siphon it into heavy sparkling wine bottles. Fit hollow-domed or blister plastic stoppers, wiring them on with a cage. Leave the bottles in a warm room for a week and then transfer them to a cool place for 6 months before drinking.

A sweet cider is best made by dissolving 1 or at the most 2 saccharin pellets per Imperial pint/550 ml (2½ cups) to the above cider at the bottling stage. Further fermentation is thus prevented and the sweetness of the cider controlled.

=Forgotten Crafts Remembered=

In the seventeenth, eighteenth and nineteenth centuries every comfortable household worthy of the name, and a good many cottages too, made and kept a stock of country-style beverages. Meads and melomels were produced, as well as home-spiced vinegars for use in cooking and at table, and alcoholic cordials, spirits and liqueurs of all kinds. It was not then illegal to distil your own spirits, and the alembic or domestic still was a common piece of equipment.

All kinds of flower waters, particularly rose water, were distilled. Lemon and orange waters and, of course, fruit juices, herbs and spices of all kinds were popular ingredients. Spices such as nutmeg, cloves and cinnamon were mixed with anise, caraway and coriander seeds. Liquorice root was added, and the whole was steeped in water and spirits then distilled and passed through saffron to give it a yellow colour. Finally it was sweetened and called *Usquebaugh* (Gaelic for water of life). Later – perhaps because the Scots made more of such waters than anyone else – one particularly potent 'water of life', flavoured with native peats and malts retained the name. The English word for it is whisky.

With a fine range of different spirits at their disposal, people made a wide range of beverages by infusing various ingredients in them. It was an ancient, inexpensive and simple activity with straightforward rules, which apply as much to today's liqueur-makers as they did to yesterday's. The recipes and methods which follow combine the best of the traditional skills with the finest of modern techniques and ingredients. The results justify the revival of a memorable craft.

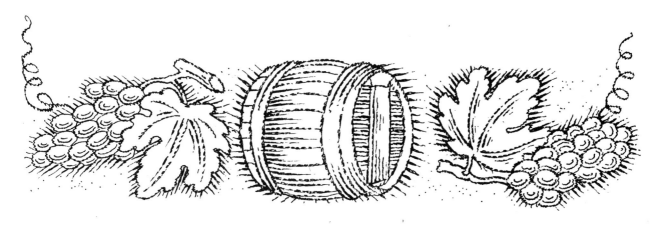

Cordials and Ratafias

Essentials

1.) *Make the infusion in stoneware jars.*
Traditionally, cast-iron pots of every shape and size were used for all cooking purposes although some copper pans were used in upper-class homes, especially in the dairy. Pewter vessels were commonly used for drinking both in the home and in the hostelries, taverns and inns. None of these vessels was suitable for use with acid fruits or for storing spiritous liquors. Earthenware jars with a lead-based glaze were equally dangerous. Nowadays, only glass, ceramic or stoneware are really safe; even modern plastics are suspect with high concentrations of alcohol, and should be avoided.

2.) *Use only the finest spirits.*
When it was common to distil your own spirits, many were so poorly made that they were positively dangerous. Paralysis, blindness, 'brain fever' could all be brought about by drinking spirits. These horrors eventually led to the law forbidding distillation in the home or without a licence. Modern spirits, commercially and accurately made, and purchased from orthodox retailers are, however, perfectly suitable as a base for cordials.

3.) *Use only the finest flowers, fruits and spices, avoiding poor quality, dry or mouldy ingredients.*
Do not be tempted to use poor ingredients on the grounds of economy; by their very nature they can never produce the best results. With spirits so highly taxed, and therefore expensive, it is a waste of money to save money on the other essentials.

4.) *Infuse the ingredients in the spirits from six to eight weeks in a tightly closed jar to prevent evaporation and in a moderately warm position.*
There have always been different schools of thought about the best length of time for infusion: some traditional cordial-makers thought that three weeks were enough, others that three months were necessary. To some extent, it depended then—as it still does now—on the strength of flavour in the ingredients and the degree of flavour required in the finished liqueur. Kilner-type jars seem to be the most suitable type of containers to use for infusion today since they are made from glass and effect an airtight seal. The temperature of the storage position is important: if it is too cold a place, it takes longer for the flavour to diffuse through the spirit; if too warm, the fruit tends to 'cook' and become so soft that it breaks up and clouds the spirit. The flavour becomes harsh, too. The jars are best stored on a shelf in a dark cupboard where the temperature range is between 59°F and 68°F/15°C and 20°C.

It goes without saying that the juiciest fruits should be infused in the strongest spirits, otherwise the result will be too weak. Filtering the infusion through several layers of cloth, to ensure a crystal bright result, is also recommended. Paper coffee filters are excellent for this purpose.

Ratafias were one of the results of such infusions and the quantities made were very substantial compared with our modern endeavours. For example an old recipe for two Imperial gallons/9 litres (10 quarts) of *Imperial Ratafia* called for:

> *2 oz of bruised kernels of peaches,*
> *apricots and nectarines*
> *5 oz of bruised bitter almonds*
> *½ pint of the best rectified spirits of wine*
> *½ drachm of essence of ambergris*
> *10 pints of malt spirits (whisky)*
> *4 pints of English Frontiniac wine (see page 88)*
> *1½ pints of distilled rose water*
> *1 lb of sugar.*

The ratafia was made by steeping the kernels and almonds in the liquor for ten days, then straining out and discarding them, before stirring in the sugar.

Imperial Ratafia was mostly used for flavouring other foods and seldom drunk by itself. The flavour of bitter almonds is not particularly pleasant in such a concentration.

Ratafia of Oranges

In comparison with some traditional drinks, this is a simple recipe. It has been reduced in scale for modern-day experiment.

Yield: 1¾ pints/1 litre (1 quart)

Imperial/metric	American
2 oranges	2 oranges
1 bottle eau de vie, vodka or gin	1 fifth grappa, vodka or gin
10 oz/300 g white sugar	1¼ cups white sugar
7 fl oz/200 ml warm water	1 scant cup warm water

Sterilize all equipment as needed. Start your records.

Thinly pare the oranges, avoiding all white pith. Chop the rind finely and infuse it in the spirit for 15 days.

Dissolve the sugar in the water and, when cool, add the expressed and strained juice of the oranges. Then bottle, seal and store in the refrigerator. Strain the parings from the spirit and discard them. Mix the flavoured spirit with the syrup, stir well and bottle.

Keep for 1 week for the ingredients to homogenize.

Ratafia of Four Fruits

This delicious ratafia is adapted from a popular eighteenth century recipe. The original recipe called for four times the quantities of ingredients given here!

Yield: about 4 pints/2.2 litres (5 pints)

Imperial/metric	American
1 lb/450 g raspberries	1 lb raspberries
1 lb/450 g blackcurrants	1 lb blackcurrants
2 lb/900 g redcurrants	2 lb redcurrants
2 lb/900 g Morello cherries	2 lb sour cherries
6 cloves	6 whole cloves
1 blade of mace	1 blade of mace
1 lb/450 g caster sugar	2 cups superfine sugar
1¾ pints/1 litre eau de vie or vodka	1 quart grappa or vodka

Sterilize all equipment as needed. Start your records.

Wash, stalk, stone (pit) and crush the fruit. Add the cloves and mace, sprinkle on the sugar, cover and leave overnight in the refrigerator.

Next day, strain out the pulp and press it dry. Measure the juice and, if the quantity exceeds 2 pints/1.2 litres (5 cups), stir in more sugar at the rate of 4 oz/115 g (½ cup) per ½ pint/300 ml (1¼ cups).

When the fruit syrup is ready, mix it with the eau de vie (grappa) and pour it into a half gallon jar or crock. Seal and leave in a cool, dark place for as long as it takes to clear. Siphon off the ratafia from the sediment.

Store it in suitable bottles for 1 year. Serve in antique or port wine glasses.

Gooseberry Ratafia

This is a modernized version of a traditional after-dinner cordial. The end result is a clear, golden drink slightly sweet and spicy, which is excellent on its own or with cheese.

Yield: 2¼ pints/1.25 litres (scant 1½ quarts)

Imperial/metric	American
2 lb/1 kg ripe gooseberries	2 lb ripe gooseberries
Small cinnamon stick	Small cinnamon stick
6 bruised cloves	6 whole bruised cloves
1 standard bottle eau de vie, vodka or gin	1 fifth grappa, vodka or gin
10 oz/300 g caster sugar	1¼ cups superfine sugar

Sterilize all equipment as needed. Start your records.

Trim the gooseberries, then wash and mash or blend them. Place the pulp in a fine mesh nylon straining bag, squeeze out all the juice and discard the pulp. Mix the gooseberry juice with the spices, spirit and about 4 oz/115 g (½ cup) of sugar. Seal and leave in a cool dark place for 1 month.

Filter or siphon the clear liquid off the sediment. Stir in the remaining sugar until it has dissolved, and then bottle.

Keep for a further month, or longer. The ratafia improves with age.

Mixed Fruit Cordial

Yield: 3 pints/1.75 litres (scant 2 quarts)

Imperial/metric	American
1 lb/450 g strawberries	1 lb strawberries
1 lb/450 g raspberries	1 lb raspberries
1 lb/450 g Morello cherries	1 lb sour cherries
½ lb/225 g blackcurrants	½ lb blackcurrants
1 standard bottle eau de vie or vodka	1 fifth grappa or vodka
Sugar to your taste—about 6 oz/175 g	About ¾ cup superfine sugar

Sterilize all equipment as needed. Start your records.

Clean and crush the soft fruit, stalk and open the cherries, leaving the stones (pits) in. Sprinkle with 4 oz/115 g (½ cup) caster (superfine) sugar and leave in a cool place overnight.

Next day, put the mashed fruit into a crock or jar and pour on the spirit, stirring to mix. Seal and leave it in a cool dark place for 5 days, shaking it each day.

Strain out the fruit through a filter bag into a second container, letting it drain dry. Do not press. Taste the cordial and, if necessary, stir in more sugar to your taste then bottle and label it.

Store the cordial for 3 or 4 weeks until it is clear.

Sir Walter Raleigh's Cordial Water

Yield: 1½ pints/900 ml (scant 1 quart)

Imperial/metric
5 lb/2.25 kg ripe
  strawberries
1 standard bottle eau de vie
  or vodka
Honey or sugar to taste

American
5 lb ripe strawberries
1 fifth grappa or vodka
Honey or sugar to taste

Sterilize all equipment as needed. Start your records.

Clean and hull the strawberries, then mash them to a pulp. Put the mashed strawberries into a crock or other container and pour on the spirit. Seal the container and leave it in a cool, dark place for 5 days, shaking it daily. Strain out the strawberry pulp and discard it.

Sweeten the liquor with honey or sugar to taste—start with no more than a tablespoonful/15 ml and repeat as necessary to achieve the desired degree of sweetness.

Bottle the cordial and and set aside for a few weeks, until the liquor has cleared. The cordial improves with age.

Blackcurrant Cordial

This is another strong cordial, nearly 35 per cent alcohol by volume. Serve it in liqueur glasses or dilute it with cold white table wine or soda water to make a long drink in summer.

Yield: 35 fl oz/1 litre (2 pints)

Imperial/metric
½ lb/225 g blackcurrants
1 standard bottle eau de vie,
  vodka, gin or rectified
  spirits
About ½ lb/225 g caster
  sugar

American
½ lb blackcurrants
1 fifth grappa, vodka or gin
About 1 cup superfine sugar

Sterilize all equipment as needed. Start your records.

Select the biggest and ripest currants you can find. Stalk them, wash carefully and mash. Place the mashed fruit in a suitable container, pour on the spirit and stir well. Seal and leave in a cool dark place for 10 weeks, shaking the container every few days to extract the colour and the juice.

Strain out and drain the currants and measure the quantity of liquor. To each 1 pint/550 ml (2½ cups), add 6 oz/175 g (¾ cup) of caster (superfine) sugar. Stir gently to dissolve the sugar, return it to the container and leave it in the same cool dark place until it is bright.

Pour the clear cordial into suitable bottles, filtering out the sediments. Seal and label. Keep this cordial for 1 month before drinking it.

White Currant Shrub

This recipe produces a colourless shrub with a subtle flavour.

Yield: about 2 pints/1.2 litres (2½ pints)

Imperial/metric	American
1½ lb/675 g white currants	1½ lb white currants
¼ lb/115 g caster sugar	½ cup superfine sugar
1 standard bottle white rum	1 fifth white rum

Sterilize all equipment. Start your records.

Stalk, wash and crush the currants, sprinkle on the sugar, cover the container and leave it in a cool place overnight.

Next day, pour on the spirit, seal the container and leave for 2 days, shaking the container several times. Strain out and drain the currants through a jelly bag, pressing them gently with the back of a wooden spoon. Bottle and seal the shrub, then store in a cool dark place until it is bright.

When the shrub has cleared, decant into fresh bottles, filtering out the sediment. Store in a cool place for 1 month before drinking.

Kirsch

This is a strong liqueur (about 32 per cent alcohol) with a pronounced cherry flavour. It should be served in liqueur glasses.

Yield: 1¾ pints/1 litre (1 quart)

Imperial/metric	American
2 lb/900 g Morello cherries	2 lb sour cherries
10 oz/300 g caster sugar	1¼ cups superfine sugar
1 standard bottle eau de vie, white rum or vodka	1 fifth grappa, white rum or vodka

Sterilize all equipment as needed. Start your records.

Wash the cherries, cut off half the stalks and split the fruit open, leaving the stones (pits). Place them in a suitable container, sprinkling each layer with sugar. Cover and leave overnight in a cool place.

Next day, pour on the spirit, stir well, seal and store in a cool dark place for 6 months. Shake the container occasionally to distribute the colour and flavour. Strain out and drain the cherries. Pour the kirsch into another container, seal and store until it is bright.

Pour into bottles, filtering out the sediment. Store in a cool place for at least 1 month before drinking.

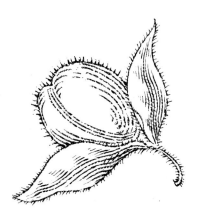

Curaçao

Although gin or vodka may be used in this recipe, the flavour is best with French eau de vie or Italian grappa.

Yield: about 2 pints/1.2 litres (2½ pints)

Imperial/metric	American
4 lemons	*4 lemons*
4 oranges	*4 oranges*
Small cinnamon stick	*Small cinnamon stick*
4 cloves	*4 whole cloves*
1 standard bottle eau de vie, gin or vodka	*1 fifth grappa, gin or vodka*
10 oz/300 g caster sugar	*1¼ cups superfine sugar*

Sterilize all equipment as needed. Start your records.

Thinly pare the fruit, avoiding all white pith, and chop finely. Express and strain the juice and set aside. Put the chopped rind, fruit juice, cinnamon, cloves and spirit into a suitable container. Stir in the sugar gently until it is all dissolved. Seal and store somewhere accessible for a month. Shake the contents once or twice each day to distribute the flavours.

After a month, strain out the spices and fruit through a filter and pour the Curaçao into suitable bottles. Seal and label. Store in a cool place for 1 month.

Mint Liqueur

Garden mint is the flavouring used for this popular liqueur, but spearmint or peppermint may also be used.

Yield: 1¾ pints/1 litre (1 quart)

Imperial/metric	American
1 oz/25 g garden mint leaves	*1 oz fresh mint leaves*
1 standard bottle eau de vie or vodka	*1 fifth grappa or vodka*
1 lb/450 g caster sugar	*2 cups superfine sugar*
½ fl oz/15 ml glycerine	*1 tbsp glycerine*

Sterilize equipment as needed. Start your records.

Select fresh young mint, remove the leaves and chop them finely. Alternatively, freeze the leaves for 24 hours in a polythene (plastic) bag, then reduce them to small particles between your fingers. Place the leaves in a suitable container. Pour the spirit over them, stir well, seal and leave for 1 week in a cool dark place, where the container can be shaken daily.

Strain out the mint through a fine nylon strainer or cloth, stir in the sugar until it is dissolved, then add the glycerine. If you so wish, add a few drops of green food colouring until the colour pleases you. In order to avoid too violent a green, this is best done drop by drop, since you can always add one more drop but can never reduce the colour!

Pour the liqueur into suitable bottles, seal and label. Store for a few months to allow the flavours to homogenize.

—Liqueurs and Fruit Brandies—

When French brandy was very cheap it was frequently used not only as an additive to oversweet, low alcohol wines but also as a base for fruit brandies. The method for making these was very simple and produced a very acceptable liqueur. Selected fruit, such as Morello cherries, peaches, apricots, strawberries, raspberries, and so on, were prepared and steeped in sugar and brandy for a few months. After the fruit juices had flavoured the brandy, the fruit pulp was withdrawn and the liqueur consumed.

Modern brandies are usually coloured and flavoured with caramel. Unfortunately this overpowers the fruit flavour—especially the subtle ones. You can buy in any wine shop in France, however, and in certain high quality shops elsewhere, an uncoloured, unflavoured brandy called Eau de Vie pour les Fruits. In Italy they make a similar uncoloured brandy called grappa. This makes an excellent modern base for fruit brandies.

Preparation Preparation of the fruit used varies slightly. **Morello cherries,** for example, should be stalked, washed and pricked all over with a sharp fork or needle to allow the juice to get out. Each cherry could also be cut in half. **Peaches and apricots** need to be peeled and stoned (pitted), and then cut up into thin slices. **Strawberries** should be stalked, washed and cut up. **Oranges** are best washed then rubbed over with sugar lumps until all the zest from the skin has been absorbed, the sugar lumps are then added together with the expressed and strained juice. **Loganberries, mulberries** and **raspberries** may be left whole because of their thin skins, but you can also cut them in two with a sharp knife. Fresh **pineapple** needs to be trimmed, peeled and cut into small dice-size pieces. **Dessert gooseberries** must be trimmed and quartered.

The amount of fruit used varies with its quality in a particular season, and how strongly flavoured you wish the brandy to be. Experience shows that about 1 lb/450 g of fruit to the standard bottle (1 fifth) of spirit is enough.

Large kilner-type jars are the most suitable containers in which to prepare fruit brandies. The jar and lid should be first washed and sterilized and the rubber ring checked for efficiency. If it is even slightly perished it should be replaced by a new one.

In the absence of eau-de-vie or grappa, vodka is the next best spirit base because it is colourless and flavourless. Other spirits are not generally suitable although several of them can be used for certain fruits. Gin, for example, is excellent with sloes and oranges.

Glycerine, in the proportion of ½ fl oz/15 ml per bottle of spirit, adds significant smoothness to liqueurs. Up to twelve drops of capsicum tincture may also be used. This adds some additional warmth or glow to the 'farewell' of the liqueurs after they have been swallowed. Both these substances are certainly worth adding, for they add that little extra polish that makes a subtle rather than a profound difference.

Storage and serving It is worth looking out for decorative bottles in which to store your liqueurs. Alternatively, store them in whatever bottle is most convenient and look around for some small decanters from which you can serve them. Silver mountings and delicately cut or engraved glass greatly enhance the appearance of the drinks.

All liqueurs should finish with a crystal bright clarity, although they may throw a thin deposit in their storage vessel. It is often useful to store them in relatively small bottles, the contents of which can be comfortably consumed within two or three weeks at the most. Although the weakest is around 20 per cent alcohol in volume and the strongest is around 35 per cent, they do not keep for ever once opened and will slowly deteriorate. Do not leave them for months on end in a centrally heated dining-room and expect them to remain perfectly fresh!

Once opened, it is best to keep the bottle, well sealed, in the refrigerator, since this keeps the liqueur in the best condition for a longer period. Take the bottle out a few hours before serving to remove any sense of chill.

Fruit Brandy

This basic recipe can be used for a wide variety of fruits.

Yield: 1¾ pints/1 litre (1 quart)

Imperial/metric	American
1 lb/450 g fruit	1 lb fruit
6 to 9 oz/175 to 250 g caster sugar	¾ to a generous cup superfine sugar
1 standard bottle eau de vie or vodka	1 fifth grappa or vodka
½ fl oz/15 ml glycerine	1 tbsp glycerine
12 drops capiscum tincture (if available)	12 drops capiscum tincture (if available)

Sterilize equipment as needed. Start your records.

Clean, peel, stone (pit) and cut up the fruit as required. Place the prepared fruit in a jar or crock in layers, covering each layer with caster (superfine) sugar. (The precise amount of sugar used will depend on the ripeness and sweetness of the fruit and your own palate—ripe apricots and peaches clearly need less than raspberries and loganberries.) Pour on the spirits, seal the jar and shake it gently to help dissolve the sugar and diffuse the juice.

Store the labelled jar in a cool dark place for 3 months, giving it an occasional shake to distribute the fruit flavour.

After 3 months, strain off the fruit brandy into suitable bottles, seal, label and store for another month before serving—in moderation!

Raspberry Gin

This old recipe makes a very pleasant drink with an alcohol content of about 20 per cent.

Yield: 2 full bottles

Imperial/metric	American
10 oz/300 g ripe raspberries	10 oz ripe raspberries
1 standard bottle gin	1 fifth gin
1 pint/550 ml hot water	2½ cups hot water
10 oz/300 g white sugar	1¼ cups white sugar

Sterilize equipment as needed. Start your records.

Wash the raspberries and either leave whole or cut in half. Place the raspberries in a jar or crock, pour on the gin, seal and leave in a warm place for 1 week, shaking it every day. Dissolve the sugar in hot water until it is transparent then leave it to cool.

Pour the raspberry gin through a fine strainer on to the cool syrup and stir well. Bottle, seal and label. Store for a few weeks so that the spirit and syrup can homogenize.

Sloe Gin

This is a very popular old country recipe. The quantity of sloes to use varies according to different palates, but the following makes a very smooth drink.

Yield: 1⅛ bottles

Imperial/metric	American
12 oz/350 g selected sloes	*¾ lb selected sloes*
6 oz/175 g caster sugar	*¾ cup superfine sugar*
1 standard bottle gin	*1 fifth gin*

Sterilize equipment as needed. Start your records.

Use the largest and blackest sloes you can find. Stalk, wash and prick them all over. Place the sloes in a jar in layers, covering each layer with sugar. Pour on the gin. Leave for 3 months, shaking occasionally to distribute the flavour.

Strain out and discard the sloes. Bottle, seal and label. Store for 1 year to mature.

Variations: If you use a sweet gin, the amount of sugar in the recipe can be reduced. If the final result is not as sweet as you would like, the gin may be sweetened before serving.

Orange Gin

Yield: 1⅛ bottles

Imperial/metric	American
1 Seville orange	*1 Seville orange*
1 sweet orange	*1 sweet orange*
½ lb/225 g sugar	*1 cup white sugar*
1 standard bottle gin	*1 fifth gin*

Sterilize equipment as needed. Start your records.

Very thinly pare the orange rinds, avoiding all white pith, and chop finely. Express and strain the juice. Place the orange rind and juice in a jar or crock and add the sugar. Pour on the gin, stirring gently until all the sugar is dissolved and the spirit is clear. Seal and store in a cool dark place for 1 week, shaking it gently each day.

Strain through a fine nylon strainer into suitable bottles, seal and label. Store for 1 year before drinking.

Blackcurrant Rum

White rum must be used in this recipe, as coloured rum contains caramel.

Yield: 1⅓ bottles

Imperial/metric	American
½ lb/225 g blackcurrants	*½ lb blackcurrants*
½ lb/225 g caster sugar	*1 cup superfine sugar*
1 standard bottle white rum	*1 fifth white rum*

Sterilize equipment as needed. Start your records.

Stalk, wash and mash the blackcurrants. Place the fruit and sugar in a jar or crock, pour on the rum and stir until the sugar is dissolved. Seal and leave for 1 week, gently shaking the jar daily.

Strain out, drain and gently press the fruit, pour the rum into suitable bottles, seal and label. Store for 1 year before drinking.

Coffee Rum

Yield: 1 quart/2.25 litres (2½ pints)

Imperial/metric
½ pint/300 ml strong black
  coffee
10 oz/300 g soft brown
  sugar
1 standard bottle rum

American
1¼ cups strong black coffee
1¼ cups light brown sugar
1 fifth rum

Sterilize equipment as needed. Start your records.

Use the best quality of freshly ground coffee that you can obtain. Place a level tablespoonful/15 ml in a jug, pour on half a pint (1¼ cups) of hot water and leave for 5 minutes. Place the sugar in a suitable container and pour the coffee through a fine nylon strainer on to it. Stir gently until the sugar is dissolved. Cover and leave to cool. Mix in the rum and pour into suitable bottles, seal and label. Keep for 1 year before serving.

Advocaat

Ladies were reputedly especially fond of this drink—particularly when out for a gossip! It should be served in port wine glasses.

Yield: 1 bottle

Imperial/metric
½ pint/300 ml water
¼ lb/115 g white sugar
1 vanilla pod
6 egg yolks
½ standard bottle vodka

American
1¼ cups water
½ cup white sugar
1 vanilla bean
6 egg yolks
1 pint vodka

Sterilize equipment as needed. Start your records.

Bring the water, sugar and vanilla pod to the boil and stir until the sugar is dissolved. Remove the vanilla pod. Separate the eggs. Beat the egg yolks thoroughly, and VERY SLOWLY add the hot syrup, beating the eggs vigorously so that they do not curdle. This must be done carefully; if the egg yolks boil, they will scramble, with disastrous results! Stir in the vodka and bottle at once.

Seal and label and keep in a cool dark place. Store for 1 week before serving.

Variations: Other recipes include the zest of a lemon rind instead of vanilla, 5 oz/150 g instead of ¼ lb/115 g sugar; rum or brandy instead of vodka; and so on. Others replace half the water with fresh single (light) cream or evaporated unsweetened milk to make an even richer drink.

Meads and Melomels

Wild honey, if it may so be called, is certainly the oldest sweetening agent known to mankind and is probably the basis of his oldest alcoholic drink—mead. Honey left in a gourd and diluted with water would soon begin to ferment from wild yeasts. Drunk a few days later, it would taste quite different to an unsophisticated palate. There seem good reasons for believing that mead was made at first in this way, perhaps as much as two thousand years before grape wine.

As civilization developed, bees were 'domesticated' not only for their honey but also for their wax, from which candles were made. The Christian Church was especially involved and monasteries and convents kept many bee hives to make candles for use in church. The honey was not only used for sweetening cakes and puddings, but also for making mead. The monks, in particular, especially in non-wine growing areas, had a traditional reputation for being great meadmakers and drinkers. It is fair to say that they also did much to improve the strain of bees kept, the hives in which bees lived and the methods of extracting the honey. Indeed, they founded and developed the craft of apiculture.

Basically, mead is a wine produced by the fermentation of diluted honey. It is made in exactly the same way, with the same equipment and many of the same essential ingredients as wine (see pages 20 to 47). The ingredient which makes mead different is honey. Honey is made by bees from the nectar of flowers and it follows that, as flowers have different perfumes, so their nectar will have different flavours and will make honeys of varying flavours. These in turn will produce quite different meads. Perhaps the most obvious difference is mead made from honey produced from the nectar of orange blossoms, compared with mead made from honey produced from the nectar of clover or lucerne. The flower taste comes right through into the finished mead. When making mead, then, select your honey with some care for when the sugar is fermented the flavour will be exposed. The mild-flavoured honeys such as clover, lucerne and lime are best for simple straightforward meads to be drunk with food; stronger flavoured honey such as heather is best reserved for strong, sweet mead to be drunk as a dessert beverage after a meal; blended honeys are best for *melomels* and *metheglins*.

The honey solution from the washing of the combs may also be used for making mead. It should be pasteurized at 122°F/50°C for a quarter of an hour, passed through a fine strainer and allowed to cool. Measure the specific gravity of the solution with a hydrometer—a reading between 1.080 and 1.090 is required. It may be necessary to stir in some additional honey to achieve these figures, which are essential to produce a mead that contains between 10 and 12 per cent alcohol when fermentation is complete.

White crystalline honey is generally regarded as the most suitable for dry, light table meads, while the brown liquid honey is regarded as the most suitable for sweet and strong meads. Three-quarters of a jar of honey is fermentable, but the remaining quarter consists of water. Honey lacks the acid needed to effect a good fermentation and flavour, and also the nitrogen so essential for the yeast. Without nitrogen, fermentation will be slow, little alcohol will be formed and the mead will be very sweet. Modern meadmakers therefore, always add sufficient acid and nutrient with the activated yeast.

Light dry meads are excellent when served nicely chilled with food such as fish, poultry, pork and particularly ham. If the flavour is not obtrusive, dry meads also make an interesting and unusual aperitif.

Light and delicate *melomels* also make good companions with food. The red melomels may be served with lamb or beef dishes depending on the fruit used. Strong and heavy melomels should be served sweet and free from chill as an after-dinner social drink.

Strong meads such as *hypocras* and *metheglin* are best served after a meal or as a speciality between meals. All meads are delicious, especially when well made, adequately matured and properly served.

Mead

The following recipe will make a light dry mead, which is best served lightly chilled as a dinner wine.

Yield: 6 bottles

Imperial/metric	American
3 lb/1.35 kg white crystalline honey (such as clover or lime)	3 lb white crystalline honey (such as clover or lime)
6½ pints/4.2 litres soft warm water	4 quarts soft warm water
¾ oz/20 g citric acid (or the juice of 3 or 4 lemons)	¾ oz (2 tbsp) citric acid or the juice of 3 or 4 lemons)
1 tsp/5 g diammonium phosphate crystals	1 tsp diammonium phosphate crystals
Maury yeast or all-purpose wine yeast	All-purpose wine yeast
Campden tablets	Campden tablets

Sterilize all equipment as needed. Start your records.

Dissolve the honey in warm water 122°F/50°C with the acid and diammonium phosphate crystals. Cover and set aside until the water has cooled.

Add the activated yeast and pour the mixture into a fermentation jar. Fit an airlock and ferment at a temperature of about 68-75°F/ 20-24°C until finished.

When the fermentation is over, move the jar to a cool place for a few days, then siphon the clearing mead into a storage jar containing 1 crushed Campden tablet. When the mead is bright, siphon it into wine bottles, cork, label and store.

Leave for at least 1 year, preferably 2, before drinking.

Variations: To make *medium sweet mead*, use 4 lb/1.8 kg of honey and, when the specific gravity has fallen to 1.010 on the hydrometer, terminate the fermentation with 1 g of potassium sorbate *and* 1 crushed Campden tablet. Clear and bottle the mead as indicated above.

To make a *strong sweet mead*, use 5 lb/2.5 kg honey and reduce the water to 6 Imperial pints/3.5 litres (7½ pints). Fermentation will be slow and will eventually stop, leaving a residue of honey.

To make an alternative *strong sweet mead* ferment 3 lb/1.35 kg honey then, when fermentation slows down, stir in another 1 lb/450 g. Repeat this process with ½ lb/225 g honey and if necessary a further ½ lb/225 g. When fermentation finally finishes, stir in sufficient honey to sweeten to suit your taste. The result is a very strong mead containing 16 or 17 per cent alcohol and as sweet as you choose. Rack it from its sediment and when the mead is bright, rack it again. Long storage is essential for this mead, between 3 and 5 years or more.

Sparkling mead can be made from light dry mead when it is crystal bright and about 6 months old. Stir in 3 oz/75 g honey per Imperial gallon/ 4.5 litres (5 quarts) together with a Champagne wine yeast and nutrient. Fit an airlock to the jar and, when it is fermenting, pour it into sterilized Champagne bottles. Leave a headspace above the mead of about 2 in/5 cm and secure the stopper with a wire cage. Label the bottles and place them in a warm place (70°F or 21°C) for a week while the sugar in the honey is fermented. Store the bottles on their sides for at least 1 year before disgorging the sediment, as described on page 42.

Sparkling mead may be served cool and fresh on any occasion. Serve it in tall tulip-shaped glasses and it will give great pleasure to all.

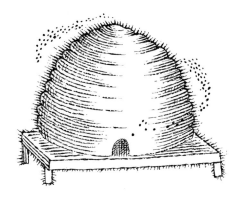

Mead, its origins buried in history, can be brewed in many different varieties of flavour according to the type of honey used.

Melomel

Melomels are meads flavoured with fruit juices. They are something of an acquired taste to the uninitiated. An ordinary fruit must can easily be turned into a melomel by adding honey rather than sugar. Remember that 25 per cent more honey than sugar will be needed and just a little less water. Alternatively, blended fresh fruit juice may be added to a mead must. The quantity of water used must be reduced proportionately. Melomels often taste better when they are served slightly sweet rather than completely dry. The acid, too, should be reduced a little when sharp tasting fruits are used.

Yield: 6 bottles

Imperial/metric	American
3½ lb/1.6 kg light honey	3½ lb light honey
7 pints/4 litres warm water	8¾ pints warm water
1 lb/450 g raspberries, red currants, strawberries etc.	1 lb raspberries, red currants, strawberries etc.
½ oz/15 g citric acid	½ oz citric acid
1 tsp/5 ml grape tannin	1 tsp grape tannin
Sauternes wine yeast and nutrient	Sauternes wine yeast and nutrient
Campden tablets	Campden tablets

Sterilize all equipment as needed. Start your records.

Dissolve the honey in the water, wash and crush the fruit and add it to the honey solution together with the acid and tannin. Cover and set aside until the must is cool.

Add the activated yeast and nutrient and ferment the pulp for 4 days, keeping it submerged. Strain out, press and discard the fruit.

Pour the must into a fermentation jar, fit an airlock and ferment on until the specific gravity measures 1.010. Siphon the clearing melomel into a sterilized jar and terminate the fermentation with 1 g potassium sorbate and 1 crushed Campden tablet. Leave in a cold place until the melomel is clear, then rack again.

Store for at least a year before drinking.

Variations: Melomel can also be made with flowers. Use the same quantity of flowers and prepare them in the same way as for flower wines (see pages 84 to 90). Replace the fruit and water in the recipe above with the flower water and ferment in the jar in the same way.

Cyser

Cyser is mead flavoured with apples. The following recipe makes a light, dry cyser that can be sweetened later if so desired. Serve chilled as a dry white table wine.

Yield: 6 bottles

Imperial/metric	American
8 lb/3.6 kg mixed cooking and eating apples	8 lb mixed cooking and eating apples
4 pints/2.25 litres water	5 pints water
Juice only of half a large lemon	Juice only of half a large lemon
Champagne wine yeast and nutrient	Champagne wine yeast and nutrient
2 lb/900 g white honey	2 lb white honey
Campden tablets	Campden tablets

Sterilize all equipment as needed. Start your records.

Wash and crush or chop the apples (skin and core included). Drop them at once into the water, which should already contain 1 crushed Campden tablet and the juice of half a lemon. Cover and leave for 24 hours.

Next day, add the activated yeast and nutrient and ferment the pulp for 5 days, pressing it down each day. Strain out, press dry and discard the fruit. Stir in the honey, pour the must into a fermentation jar, top up with cold boiled water, fit an airlock and ferment out.

Move the jar to a cool place for a few days while the sediment settles, then siphon the cyser into a sterilized jar containing 1 crushed Campden tablet. Cork, label and store in a cool place until bright, then bottle.

Store for 1 or 2 years before drinking.

Metheglin

Metheglin is mead flavoured with herbs or spices in the same way as hypocras. It is best made from strong-flavoured honey at the rate of at least 4 lb/1.8 kg honey to the Imperial gallon/4.5 litres (5 quarts). This produces a strong mead with a fair amount of body to balance the flavour. It should be served sweet and, like hypocras, tastes very good when served warm.

Yield: 6 bottles

Imperial/metric	American
4 lb/1.8 kg strong-flavoured honey	4 lb dark honey
6 pints/3.4 litres warm water	7½ pints warm water
¾ oz/20 g citric acid	¾ oz citric acid
1 tsp/5 ml grape tannin	1 tsp grape tannin
Sauternes wine yeast and nutrient	Sauternes wine yeast and nutrient
1 lemon	1 lemon
Bouquet garni of mixed herbs (balm, mace, marjoram, rosemary) or mixed spices (root ginger, cloves, allspice, cinnamon)	Bouquet garni of mixed herbs (balm, mace, marjoram, rosemary) or mixed spices (ginger root, cloves, allspice, cinnamon)
Campden tablets	Campden tablets

Sterilize all equipment as needed. Start your records.

Dissolve the honey in the water, add the citric acid, tannin and, when cool, the activated yeast and nutrient. Pour this must into a fermentation jar.

Thinly pare and chop the lemon rind, avoiding all white pith, and place it in a muslin or nylon bag with the bouquet garni of herbs or spices. Suspend this in the jar. Express the juice of the lemon and strain this into the jar. Fit an airlock and leave the jar in a warm position.

Remove the bag of flavouring after the first week or as soon as enough flavouring has been extracted to suit your taste. Check the specific gravity from time to time and, when a reading of 1.016 is reached, siphon the metheglin into a clear jar containing 1 g of potassium sorbate and 1 crushed Campden tablet. Move the jar to a cool place and rack again as soon as the metheglin has thrown a further deposit. When the metheglin is clear, rack once more.

Store for at least 1 year (preferably longer) before bottling.

Note: Use as many different sweet herbs as possible and not too much of any single herb. Savoury herbs such as parsley, sage and thyme are not very successful and should therefore be avoided. Be gentle with spices. You can add more when the metheglin is finished but you cannot reduce too strong a flavour except by blending with a bland mead.

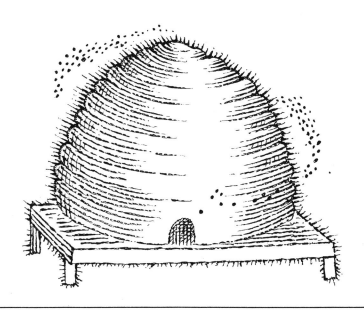

Pyment

Pyment probably originated in the time of the Ancient Greeks, when honey was added to the rather poor grape wine to improve the flavour. Today, pyment is made from grape juice and mead. Black or white grapes may be used, but if they are very sharp, then the quantity of acid should be reduced. Allowance may have to be made for their juice content by marginally reducing or increasing the quantity of water used in the following recipe.·

Yield: 6 bottles

Imperial/metric	American
10 lb/4.5 kg black or white grapes	10 lb black or white grapes
1 lb/450 g light honey	1 lb light honey
About 1¾ pints/1 litre water	1 quart water
Bordeaux wine yeast and nutrient	Bordeaux wine yeast and nutrient
Campden tablets	Campden tablets

Sterilize all equipment as needed. Start your records.

Stalk, wash and crush the grapes. Place them in a bin, dissolve the honey in the water and add to the grapes. Stir in the activated wine yeast and nutrient and ferment on the pulp for 2 days if the grapes are white, for 2 days if the grapes are black and a rosé pyment is required, or for 10 days if the grapes are black and a red pyment is wanted. Keep the pulp submerged the whole time and the bin covered.

Strain out, press dry and discard the pulp. Pour the must into a fermentation jar, top up if necessary with cold boiled water, fit an airlock and ferment out. Continue as described for *Mead*.

Variations: *Hypocras,* or pyment flavoured with spices or herbs, is another interesting and very old drink. It must be made with great care, however, as hypocras tastes better to modern palates if the taste of spices or herbs is subtle rather than pronounced. Ginger, clove, cinnamon, nutmeg and allspice are the most popular spices to use, especially with the thinly pared rind of a lemon. Rosemary, balm, thyme, mint, violet leaves and strawberry leaves are the most popular herbs. To add them to the pyment, suspend a muslin or coarse nylon bag of spices or herbs in the fermenting mead for 3 days or so until sufficient flavour has been extracted.

Hypocras usually tastes better when it is served sweet rather than dry. It also tastes very good when warmed to 140°F/60°C before serving.

Country Vinegars

With the employment of so many women outside the home, there has been a greater demand from them for prepared foods and condiments. As a result, fewer families now enjoy the flavours of fruit, herb and spiced vinegars with their food. But a reaction is setting in and there is now a renewal of interest in these culinary beverages. They are not difficult to make nor do they require expensive equipment. The only major piece of equipment required to make vinegar, in fact, is a container at least twice the size of the quantity that you wish to make. Home winemakers and brewers should take care to use quite separate containers for making vinegars, and to make them in a place quite separate from where they make their beers, ciders, meads and wines. Failure to take this precaution may well result in all the alcoholic drinks becoming tainted with the vinegar smell and taste.

When making beer, cider, mead and wine, it is essential to keep vessels full and sealed from the air to avoid infection, notably from *Acetobacter,* the vinegar bacteria, which float invisibly in the air and settle on fruit juices that have already been attacked by wild yeast cells. The vinegar bacteria attack the alcohol in beer, cider, mead and wine and convert it into the sharp and distinctive acetic acid. Indeed the word 'vinegar' is derived from the French *vin aigre,* meaning sour wine. The vinegar bacteria only function in the presence of air. This is why it is essential, when making vinegar, to use a container not more than half full and which has plentiful access to fresh air at a temperature of 25 to 30°C/77 to 86°F.

In the eighteenth and nineteenth centuries, vinegar was often made in the open air, especially in fruit orchards. Casks were laid on their sides in cradles and numerous holes were drilled in the upper half of each of the end boards. The bottom half of the cask was filled with weak or diluted wine or with cider. The cask was left permanently in position. After about three months, conversion of the wine into vinegar was complete. The vinegar was drawn off through the usual tap in the bottom of one end board, into smaller casks which were filled to the bung, or into bottles which were filled and sealed.

A fresh supply of cider or diluted wine was introduced into the cask through a funnel to which was attached a tube reaching to the bottom of the cask. In this way the *Mycoderma aceti,* or mat of vinegar cells was not unduly damaged nor disturbed. The fresh liquor came in from underneath and lifted it up to the half way mark.

This principle is the one still followed today by home vinegar-makers. Use a glass or plastic container with a capacity of about 1 gallon/4.5 litres (5 quarts)—if the vessel can be kept on its side an even larger surface area becomes available to infection. The mouth of the container should be covered only with a piece of nylon or cheesecloth to keep out flies and insects but still allow air to enter.

The container should be thoroughly clean before you use it, but do not rinse it in a sulphite solution as this might inhibit the fungus.

A funnel, a piece of rubber or plastic tubing and some bottles are the only other pieces of equipment required. Half pint/300 ml (6 fl oz) screw-stoppered mineral water bottles are excellent for storing vinegar, but anything similar will do. When bottling the vinegar, sterilize the bottles with a sulphite solution as you would for beer, cider, mead or wine.

Use light ales and ciders undiluted, but dilute meads and wines with an equal quantity of cold water to reduce the alcohol content to between 5 and 6 per cent. The proportions are five measures of beer, cider or diluted mead or wine to one measure of strong, malt vinegar, preferably drawn from a cask. Simply pour the mixture into the container, cover the opening as described above and leave it in a warm and well ventilated position, preferably with access to the outside air. It should remain undisturbed for three months.

After a few days the liquid will become hazy and within a week or two little dots will be seen floating on the surface. These will eventually join up and thicken. After about three months the vinegar will begin to clear and finally will become quite bright. This indicates that all the alcohol has been converted to vinegar and that it is now ready to be drawn off and bottled.

You can accomplish this with a piece of tubing used as a siphon direct into the prepared bottles. Fill to the brim and then loosely stopper. The bottles should now be pasteurized. To do this place the bottles on a folded hand towel in the bottom of a fish kettle, preserving pan or large boiling pan. Fill the pan with water, transfer to the stove, turn the heat on. When the water comes to the boil, lower the heat so that the water continues to simmer for 20 minutes. Then turn off the heat, tighten the stoppers and remove the bottles from the pan and leave them to cool.

If another quantity of a similar vinegar is to be made at once, draw off only three-quarters of the volume and replace it through the siphon tube with the same quantity of another beer, cider or diluted wine. This method produces vinegar all of one flavour. Others can be made either by the same method, with different herbs, spices or fruits introduced, or by infusing the herbs, spices or fruits in distilled vinegar, the process used commercially.

The most popular herbs for flavouring vinegars are borage, dill, garlic, mint and tarragon. The precise quantity to use is not critical since the quality of the herb can vary as well as the individual liking for its flavour. Use about half a teacup of only one herb with half an Imperial gallon/2.25 litres (2½ quarts) of vinegar. (The herb can be left in the jar during the process.)

An alternative method of making herb vinegar is to make up a quantity of five measures of beer, cider or diluted wine with one measure of vinegar and then to divide this into suitable containers or bottles each containing a different herb. The quantity of herb used would vary with the quantity of liquid in the bottle, in the proportion mentioned in the previous paragraph. There must be at least as much air space in a bottle as there is liquid, and the bottles should be placed in an almost horizontal position to provide the largest surface area and loosely plugged with cotton wool.

The infusion method is more often used for flavouring a vinegar with fruit. Any kind of fruit may be used after it has been stalked, washed, peeled, stoned (pitted), cut up, crushed or blended. The traditional proportion is 1 lb/450 g of fruit to 1 pint/550 ml (2½ cups) of distilled vinegar. Steep the fruit in the vinegar for forty-eight hours then strain and filter it into sterilized bottles that can be kept sealed. Raspberry vinegar is the great favourite. It may be used in vinaigrettes, marinades, poaching, pickling, etc. . . .

A strong cider, mead or white wine vinegar may be used as an alternative to distilled vinegar. It should contain at least 6 per cent acetic acid. In the past many fruit vinegars were sweetened with honey or sugar and taken as a remedy for ticklish coughs and sore throats.

Making good vinegars of all kinds deserves to be restored to its former popularity. Everyone interested in country beverages should certainly 'have a go' at vinegars.

Syruped Fruit Vinegar

A tablespoonful of this vinegar may be dissolved in warm water and taken when a cough or sore throat is troublesome. It is a very old country remedy.

Yield: 2 pints/1.2 litres (5 cups)

Imperial/metric	American
1 lb/450 g fruit (blackberry, blackcurrant, raspberry)	1 lb fruit (blackberry, blackcurrant, raspberry)
1 pint/550 ml cider, mead or white wine vinegar	2½ cups cider, mead or white wine vinegar
½ lb/225 g honey	½ lb honey
1 lb/450 g sugar	2 cups sugar

Stalk, wash and crush the fruit, cover it with the vinegar, seal the container and leave it for 48 hours, agitating it occasionally. Strain through a filter but do not press the fruit. Stir in the honey and sugar and slowly heat to 176°F/85°C. Maintain this temperature for 15 minutes, removing any scum. Pour the vinegar syrup into heated bottles and seal at once.

Spiced Vinegar

Spiced vinegars are suitable for preserving fruits or vegetables, making chutneys or poaching herrings, for example, and may be made very easily.

Yield: 2 pints/1.2 litres (5 cups)

Imperial/metric	American
2 pints/1.2 litres strong pale vinegar	5 cups strong pale vinegar
¼ oz/7 g whole allspice	¼ oz whole allspice
¼ oz/7 g cinnamon stick	¼ oz cinnamon stick
⅛ oz/3.5 g whole cloves	⅛ oz whole cloves
¼ oz/7 g mace blade	¼ oz mace blade
⅛ oz/3.5 g peppercorns (black or white)	⅛ oz peppercorns (black or white)
2 bay leaves ⎫	2 bay leaves ⎫
2 cloves of garlic ⎬ optional	2 cloves of garlic ⎬ optional
(peeled) ⎭	(peeled) ⎭

Steep a solution of spices in the vinegar for 1 month in a suitable sealed container. The vessel and its lid must be impervious to acid. Care should be taken, expecially with the lid, to ensure that any metal is not exposed.

Cloves and black peppercorns tend to discolour the vinegar slightly and should be omitted if the colour of the vinegar is important to the appearance of the pickle. The container of vinegar and spices should be stored in a cool dark place and agitated every few days to distribute the flavours into the vinegar.

If such a vinegar is used to preserve fruit, notably apricots, peaches and pineapple it should be sweetened with 1 lb sugar/450 g to the pint/550 ml (2½ cups) before pouring it over the finest quality fruit, suitably prepared, i.e. peeled, stoned (pitted) and cut into appropriate-sized portions. The vessel should then be sealed and stored in a cool dark place for 1 month.

—Punches and Mixed Drinks—

In addition to the many varieties of strong drinks available, our forebears in the eighteenth and nineteenth centuries were extremely fond of mulled wines and ales in cold winter weather and cooling iced drinks in the summer. Their inventiveness knew no bounds and their hospitality was prodigious!

With all the warmed winter punches, some recipes for which follow, the temperature to which they are heated is critical. Too low, and the punch does not taste hot; too high, and the alcohol is driven off, leaving the punch weak: 140°F/60°C is just right. You really do need a kitchen thermometer to ensure the best results – punches which are hot enough and strong enough to provide that satisfying inner glow.

The cooling summer drinks should not contain too much alcohol and are best served ice-cold in long glasses. They may be ladled from a glass or silver bowl or poured from a large colourless glass jug. Several non-alcoholic recipes are included which are particularly suitable for children, or guests who are driving.

The essence of making punch is to tailor the strength and flavour of the drinks to suit the season and the company. Many of the recipes which follow recommend the use of wines you may already have made and are, therefore, ideal ways of making good use of 'bin ends'.

Red Wine Punch

This very simple recipe never fails. Elderberry wine as used here is particularly appropriate but any strong flavoured red wine will do, however. It makes a splendid accompaniment to mince pies!

Yield: 6 to 8 glasses

Imperial/metric	American
1 lemon	1 lemon
1 bottle elderberry wine	1 bottle elderberry wine
1 piece well bruised root ginger	1 piece well bruised ginger root
1 small cinnamon stick	1 small cinnamon stick
8 cloves, slightly bruised	8 cloves, slightly bruised
2 tbsp/30 ml brown sugar	2 tbsp brown sugar
1 tbsp/15 ml honey	1 tbsp honey

Pare the lemon thinly, avoiding all white pith. Express and strain the juice and set aside.

Pour the wine into a stainless steel or unchipped enamel saucepan. Add the spices, sugar, honey and lemon rind. Heat very slowly, stirring gently to dissolve the sugar and the honey. Check the temperature of the punch every minute or so and when 140°F/60°C is reached, turn off the heat. Add the lemon juice, strain out the spices and lemon rind.

Pour into a preheated jug and serve in preheated glasses.

Variations: You will find many variations on this simple recipe (including the addition of a tot of rum) but none tastes better.

Cider Punch

Yield: 1¾ pints/1 litre (1 quart)

Imperial/metric	American
½ lemon	½ lemon
1¾ pints/1 litre strong cider	1 quart strong cider
1 piece well bruised ginger	1 piece well bruised ginger
1 tbsp/15 ml honey	1 tbsp honey

Thinly pare the half lemon and express the juice.

Place the cider, ginger, lemon rind and juice in a saucepan. Heat very slowly to a temperature of 140°F/60°C then remove from the heat and stir in the honey.

Serve at once in warmed glasses.

Egg Nog Punch

Yield: about 12 glasses

Imperial/metric	American
12 large eggs	12 large eggs
6 oz/175 g caster sugar	¾ cup superfine sugar
2 pints/1.2 litres plum or damson wine	5 cups plum or damson wine
4 pints/2.4 litres milk	2½ quarts milk
Nutmeg	Nutmeg

Break the eggs into a large bowl and gradually add the sugar, beating well. Beat until the mixture is pale and slightly frothy. Gradually pour in the wine, beating constantly, then add the milk in the same way.

Serve in stemmed glasses, with a little grated nutmeg sprinkled on top of each egg nog.

Yuletide Mulled Wine

Yield: about 20 glasses

Imperial/metric	American
4 lemons	4 lemons
5 oranges	5 oranges
About 50 cloves	About 50 cloves
1½ pints/825 ml water	3¾ cups water
4 oz/115 g sugar	½ cup sugar
2 cinnamon sticks	2 cinnamon sticks
3½ pints/2 litres red grape wine	2 quarts red grape wine
¼ pint/150 ml fruit brandy	½ cup fruit brandy

Thinly pare the rinds of all the lemons and 2 oranges, avoiding all white pith. Strain and express the juice and set aside. Prick the remaining oranges all over with a fork and stud their skins decoratively with the cloves. Set aside.

Put the water into a boiling pan and add the lemon and orange juice and skins, the sugar and the cinnamon sticks. Bring to the boil, stirring occasionally. Boil for 2 minutes, then stir and set aside for 10 minutes. Strain the liquid into a jug, pressing down on the citrus skins to extract all the juice. Discard the skins and cinnamon sticks.

Pour the wine into a saucepan and add the strained sugar liquid, brandy and reserved clove-studded oranges. Heat to 140°F/60°C and do not boil.

Ladle the mulled wine into warmed glasses. If desired, the decorated oranges can be sliced and individual slices floated in the glasses.

Bragget

Yield: 2 pints/1.2 litres (2½ pints)

Imperial/metric	American
1 pint/550 ml strong ale	2½ cups strong ale
1 pint/550 ml sweet mead	2½ cups sweet mead
1 piece bruised root ginger	1 piece bruised ginger root

Slowly heat the ale, mead and ginger in a saucepan and when the temperature reaches 140°F/60°C remove from the heat and serve at once in warmed glasses.

Variations: Use a small stick of cinnamon and 6 cloves instead of the ginger.

Saxon Glory

Yield: 6 to 8 glasses

Imperial/metric	American
1 orange	1 orange
1 bottle strong sweet mead	1 bottle strong sweet mead
1 piece well bruised root ginger	1 piece well bruised ginger root
1 small cinnamon stick	1 small cinnamon stick
6 cloves, lightly bruised	6 cloves, lightly bruised
4 fl oz/115 ml brandy	½ cup brandy

Thinly pare the orange, avoiding all white pith. Express and strain the juice.

Place all the ingredients in a saucepan and slowly warm to 140°F/60°C.

Strain into warmed glasses and serve at once.

Bishop

Yield: 6 to 8 glasses

Imperial/metric	American
1 large orange	*1 large orange*
12 cloves	*12 cloves*
1 bottle strong and sweet red wine, such as plum	*1 bottle strong and sweet red wine, such as plum*
Extra sugar to taste	*Extra sugar to taste*

Wipe over the orange and stick the cloves into it round the circumference until they do not protrude. Place it in a slow oven and *gently* roast it until it is nicely brown.

Remove the orange from the oven and cut it up into its segments. Place these in a saucepan, pour on the wine and slowly heat to 140°F/60°C.

Strain into warm glasses and drink at once.

Variations: A generous tot of rum may be added if the wine is not strong enough.

Mulled Ale

Yield: 2 pints/1.2 litres (2½ pints)

Imperial/metric	American
2 pints/1.2 litres strong ale	*2½ pints strong ale*
4 fl oz/115 ml rum	*½ cup rum*
1 tbsp/15 ml caster sugar	*1 tbsp superfine sugar*
1 well-bruised root ginger	*1 well-bruised ginger root*
6 cloves, lightly bruised	*6 cloves, lightly bruised*
Grated nutmeg to taste	*Grated nutmeg to taste*

Place all the ingredients in a saucepan and heat very slowly to 140°F/60°C, stirring gently to dissolve the sugar.

Strain into warmed glasses and serve at once.

Negus

Yield: 6 to 8 glasses

Imperial/metric	American
1 lemon	*1 lemon*
1 oz/25 g lump sugar	*1 oz lump sugar*
1 bottle strong red wine, preferably elderberry	*1 bottle strong red wine, preferably elderberry*
3 oz/75 g brown sugar	*¾ cup brown sugar*
¼ small nutmeg (grated)	*¼ small nutmeg (grated)*
3 drops vanilla essence	*3 drops vanilla extract*

Wipe the lemon with a clean damp cloth and rub off all the zest with the lump sugar. Place the lumps in a saucepan with the other ingredients and slowly heat to 140°F/60°C.

Strain into warmed glasses and serve at once.

Pope's Posset

Yield: 9 to 12 glasses

Imperial/metric
2 oz /50 g sweet almonds
2 oz /50 g bitter almonds
½ pint /300 ml cold water
1 bottle sweet white wine,
such as elderflower

American
2 oz sweet almonds
2 oz bitter almonds
1¼ cups cold water
1 bottle sweet white wine,
such as elderflower

Blanch the almonds and pound them to a thin cream with a little of the water.

Place the almond mixture and the rest of the water in a saucepan and slowly bring to boiling point. Remove from the heat and strain through a thick cloth into another saucepan containing the wine. Check the temperature and if necessary bring it up to 140°F/60°C.

Pour into warmed glasses and serve at once.

Variations: Almond essence can be used in place of the almonds and water. Its flavour is very concentrated, so add it a few drops at a time to suit your taste.

Wassail Bowl

This is a modernized version of an ancient recipe which was popular as far back as the days of King John of England (he of Magna Carta fame). The name 'Wassail' is derived from the Old English **Waes Hael** *which meant 'be of good health'. Sometimes it was served in a mazer or loving cup.*

Yield: 2 pints/1.2 litres (2½ pints)

Imperial/metric
3 small cooking apples
3 oz/75 g soft brown sugar
½ bottle dry cider
12 cloves
1 tsp /5 ml powdered ginger
Grated nutmeg to taste
1 bottle apple wine

American
3 small cooking apples
½ cup soft brown sugar
½ bottle dry cider
12 cloves
1 tsp powdered ginger
Grated nutmeg to taste
1 bottle apple wine

Wash and core the apples. Fill them with brown sugar and a little cider, then push four cloves into each apple until they no longer protrude. Bake the apples until they are soft enough to mash (about 1 hour in a moderate oven).

Remove the apple skins and discard along with the cloves. Sprinkle on the powdered ginger, the rest of the sugar and a little grated nutmeg. Mash all the ingredients together, slowly adding the rest of the cider. Stir in the apple wine, then pour the liquor into a saucepan and slowly heat to 140°F/60°C, stirring gently from time to time.

Serve in a preheated bowl and pass from one merrymaker to another! Alternatively, pour into individual warmed glasses.

Orange Cup

Yield: 6 to 8 glasses

Imperial/metric
1 large sweet orange
4 sugar cubes
6 crushed ice cubes
2 fl oz/50 ml gin (optional)
1 bottle orange wine
½ pint/300 ml mineral water
  (bitter lemon)

American
1 large sweet orange
4 sugar cubes
6 crushed ice cubes
¼ cup gin (optional)
1 bottle orange wine
1¼ cups mineral water
  (bitter lemon)

Rub the zest off the orange with the sugar cubes and set them aside. Remove and discard all the pith from the orange, slice it thinly and then quarter the slices.

Put the orange, the sugar lumps, crushed ice and gin into a suitable bowl and pour on the wine. Stir gently to dissolve the sugar, then add the mineral water.

Serve immediately.

White Wine Cup

A very elegant summer cup.

Yield: 10 glasses

Imperial/metric
1 lemon
3 sugar cubes
12 crushed ice cubes
4 fl oz/115 ml gin, vodka or
  white rum
1 bottle sweet white wine,
  such as peach
6 thin *slices unpeeled*
  cucumber
1 pint/550 ml soda water

American
1 lemon
3 sugar cubes
12 crushed ice cubes
½ cup gin vodka or white
  rum
1 bottle sweet white wine,
  such as peach
6 thin *slices unpeeled*
  cucumber
2½ cups soda water

Rub the zest off the lemon with the sugar then express and strain the juice.

Put the crushed ice cubes, sugar cubes, lemon juice, gin and wine into a suitable bowl. Stir gently to dissolve the sugar, float the cucumber slices on the top and add the mineral water.

Serve immediately.

Sherry Cobbler

Yield: 8 glasses

Imperial/metric	American
2 small oranges	2 small oranges
8 sugar cubes	8 sugar cubes
16 crushed ice cubes	16 crushed ice cubes
4 tbsp/60 ml caster sugar	4 tbsp superfine sugar
8 strawberries	8 strawberries
16 raspberries	16 raspberries
1 peach	1 peach
½ small pineapple	½ small pineapple
1 bottle cold sherry-style wine	1 bottle cold sherry-style wine

Rub the zest off the oranges with the sugar cubes and set aside. Remove all the pith from the oranges, divide into segments and cut each segment into smaller pieces. Clean all the fruit. Quarter the strawberries; halve the raspberries; peel and slice the peach and cut each slice into three; peel the pineapple and cut it up into small pieces.

Divide all the ingredients into 8 glasses. Dissolve the sugar and ice in the wine and pour it over the fruit.

Serve immediately.

Pussyfoot

This is a splendid drink for a young teenage party.

Yield: 12 glasses

Imperial/metric	American
1 eating apple	1 eating apple
1 sweet orange	1 sweet orange
1 ripe peach	1 ripe peach
4 tbsp/60 ml honey	4 tbsp honey
12 large ice cubes	12 large ice cubes
2 bottles sparkling cider	2 bottles sparkling cider

Peel the fruit and cut it into small pieces.

Divide the fruit among 12 glasses. Add a teaspoonful/5 ml of thin honey and an ice cube to each glass and stir well. Top up with cider.

Serve immediately.

Honeymoon Cup

Yield: about 15 glasses

Imperial/metric	American
1 orange	1 orange
1 lemon	1 lemon
1 pear	1 pear
2 tbsp/30 ml clear honey	2 tbsp clear honey
1 bottle dry white wine such as white currant or apple	1 bottle dry white wine such as white currant or apple
4 fl oz/115 ml fruit brandy	½ cup fruit brandy
4 fl oz/115 ml light mead or pyment	½ cup light mead or pyment
1¼ pints/600 ml lemonade	3 cups lemonade
Ice cubes	Ice cubes

Slice the orange and lemon, including the skin. Peel, core and slice the pear.

Put the honey and about one-quarter of the wine into a small saucepan and warm, stirring until the honey has dissolved. Remove from the heat and pour the mixture into a punch bowl. Stir in the remaining wine, the brandy, mead and lemonade and float the fruit slices on top. Chill for at least 2 hours.

Put two or three ice cubes into individual serving glasses and ladle the chilled wine and fruit slices over them.

Mint Julep

Yield: 8 to 10 glasses

Imperial/metric
1 sprig fresh garden mint
1 bottle chilled sherry-type wine
6 crushed ice cubes
2 tbsp/30 ml thin honey
1 pint/550 ml mineral water (ginger ale)

American
1 sprig fresh garden mint
1 bottle chilled sherry-type wine
6 crushed ice cubes
2 tbsp thin honey
2½ cups mineral water (ginger ale)

Rinse the mint under the tap, remove the leaves and chop finely.

Place the chopped mint and wine in a suitable bowl and gently stir in the honey and crushed ice until they dissolve. Add the mineral water.

Serve immediately.

Elderberry Sangria

Sangria has become a favourite summer punch in recent years and no home-made wine makes it better than elderberry. Try, too, Strawberry jam or Blueberry wine for subtly different—but very delicious—tastes.

Yield: about 12 glasses

Imperial/metric
½ orange
½ lemon
5 fresh peaches or 14 oz/400 g can peach slices, drained
1¾ pints/1 litre elderberry wine
1 tbsp/15 ml sugar
½ pint/300 ml chilled soda water
Ice cubes

American
½ orange
½ lemon
5 fresh peaches or 14 oz can peach slices, drained
2 pints elderberry wine
1 tbsp sugar
1¼ cups chilled soda water
Ice cubes

Slice the citrus fruit thinly, including the skins. If using fresh peaches, slice thinly and discard the stone (pit).

Pour the wine into a tall jug. Float the fruit slices on top and stir in the sugar until it is dissolved.

Just before serving, pour over the soda water and float in the ice cubes.

Sherbet

Yield: 1½ pints/900 ml (3¾ cups)

Imperial/metric	American
¾ lb/350 g ripe strawberries	¾ lb ripe strawberries
1 lemon	1 lemon
1 orange	1 orange
1 pint/550 ml cold water	2½ cups cold water
6 oz/175 g caster sugar	¾ cup superfine sugar
1 tsp/5 ml bicarbonate of soda	1 tsp baking soda

Stalk and wash the strawberries, then crush or blend them. Thinly pare and finely chop the lemon and orange rinds. Express and strain the juice, add the water and stir in the sugar. Seal and leave in the refrigerator overnight.

Next day, strain the sherbet through a fine strainer, stir in the soda and serve at once.

Variations: Similar sherbets may be made with raspberries, peaches, pineapples, and so on.

Welsh Nectar

Serve this slightly alcoholic beverage well chilled.

Yield: 1 gallon/4.5 litres (5 quarts)

Imperial/metric	American
2 lemons	2 lemons
½ lb/225 g seedless raisins	½ lb golden raisins
½ lb/225 g soft brown sugar	1⅓ cups soft brown sugar
1 gallon/4.5 litres boiling water	5 quarts boiling water
Ale yeast	Ale yeast
1 tbsp/15 ml thin honey	1 tbsp thin honey

Thinly pare and finely chop the lemon rinds. Express and strain the juice and set aside. Wash and chop the raisins.

Place the chopped rinds and raisins in a suitable container, add the sugar and pour on the water. Stir well until the sugar is dissolved. Cover and leave to cool.

Add the lemon juice and ale yeast, replace the cover and leave in a warm room until fermentation finishes. Move the container to a cold place for 24 hours then siphon off the sediment into beer bottles, dividing the honey dissolved in a bottle of the liquid equally between them. Seal securely and store for 2 days in a warm room.

This beverage should be drunk within a few days as it will not keep.

Raspberryade

Yield: 3 bottles

Imperial/metric
1 lb /450 g redcurrants
½ lb /225 g raspberries
2½ pints /1.4 litres cold
  water
1 lb /450 g white sugar

American
1 lb redcurrants
½ lb raspberries
6 cups cold water
2 cups white sugar

Stalk and wash the fruit then crush or blend it and place it in a saucepan with the water.

Place the pan on the heat, stir in the sugar and slowly heat to a temperature of 176°F/80°C. Maintain this temperature for 15 minutes then strain out and drain the solids through fine nylon.

Pour into sterilized bottles, seal and leave them to cool, then move them to the refrigerator.

Serve cold as a drink or freeze in lollipop moulds.

Lemonade

Yield: 33 fl oz/about 1 litre (4 cups)

Imperial/metric
3 fresh lemons
3 oz /75 g white sugar
¼ oz /7 g cream of tartar
1½ pints /900 ml boiling
  water

American
3 fresh lemons
⅓ cup white sugar
¼ oz cream of tartar
3¾ cups boiling water

Thinly pare and finely chop the lemon rinds. Express the juice and set aside.

Place the lemon rinds, sugar and cream of tartar in a bowl. Add the boiling water, stir to dissolve the sugar, cover and leave to cool. Add the lemon juice and pour the lemonade through a fine strainer into sterilized bottles. Seal and chill in the refrigerator for 1 hour, then serve.

Variations: For a 'fizzy' lemonade, use only 1 pint/550 ml of water and, when serving, add ½ pint/300 ml of gassy soda water.

For orangeade, follow the above recipe but use 3 sweet oranges. The beverage is improved by the addition of 1 lemon.

Glossary of Terms Used

Acid — The sharp taste of fruits and liquids due to the presence of citric, malic or tartaric acid.

Airlock — A device used to exclude air while permitting gas formed during fermentation to escape.

Alcohol — In the context of this book the word alcohol refers to ethyl alcohol, the spirit that is present in beer, cider, mead and wine and that is added to liqueurs of all kinds.

Campden tablet — The proprietary name for 0.44 g of compressed sodium metabisulphite. One tablet dissolved in one Imperial gallon/4.5 litres (5 quarts) of a liquid releases 50 parts per million of sulphur dioxide. See also SULPHITE.

Carbon dioxide — The gas given off during the fermentation of sugars into beer, cider, mead and wines.

Dry — A beverage in which there is a lack of sweetness. The opposite of sweet.

Enzyme — A substance which acts as a catalyst in specific circumstances. Each enzyme can cause, by its very presence, a single change in a substance, without being changed itself. The name of an enzyme always ends with the letters 'ase', e.g. diastase, maltase, sucrase, zymase.

Fermentation — The processs in which yeast converts the sugar in a liquid to alcohol and carbon dioxide.

Ferment on — Continue the fermentation after the removal of pulp or the addition of sugar.

Fermentation-on-the-pulp — Fermentation in the presence of crushed fruit, etc. to extract colour and soluble ingredients.

Ferment out — Continue the fermentation until all the sugar has been converted to alcohol and carbon dioxide.

Hydrometer — An instrument that, in the context of this book, measures the weight of sugar in a liquid.

Invert sugar — The name given to a mixture of fructose and glucose after they have been separated in ordinary household sugar (sucrose).

Maturation The ageing of a beer, cider, mead or wine to the point at which it is most pleasant to drink.

Must The name given to a liquid, with or without solids, before it is fermented into cider, mead or wine.

Nutrient Salts of ammonia added to provide nitrogen for the yeast, e.g. ammonium sulphate and/or diammonium phosphate. Sometimes a few milligrams of vitamin B_1 are also added.

Pectic enzyme An enzyme in powder or liquid form which is added to a fruit must to break down the pectin in the fruit. It improves juice extraction and prevents pectic haze in the finished wine.

Rack The process of removing a clear beer, cider, mead or wine from a sediment formed during fermentation or maturation. Usually performed with the aid of a siphon.

Sediment The dross of insoluble particles and yeast cells that collect in the bottom of a container of beer, cider, mead and wine. It can be pasty, flocculent or sandy.

Siphon A length of hose used to transfer a liquid from one vessel to another without disturbing the sediment.

Specific gravity The weight of a given volume of a liquid compared with same volume of water at a temperature of 59°F/15°C.

Starter bottle A bottle containing water, fruit acid, sugar and nutrient in which dormant yeast cells are re-activated.

Sulphite The abbreviated name of sodium or potassium metabisulphite. Used in solution, often with citric acid, to sterilize equipment and ingredients and to prevent oxidation (browning).

Tannin A bitter substance found in grape stalks, pips and skins that gives character and firmness to a wine.

Wort A solution of maltose and hop flavouring made prior to fermentation into beer.

Yeast Microscopic botanical cells that cause fermentation. The yeasts referred to in this book are called *Saccharomyces*—meaning sugar fungi. There are numerous strains of the main variety *Saccharomyces cerevisiae* (beer yeast) and of its major sub-variety *Saccharomyces cerevisiae elipsoideus* (wine yeast).

Sugar & Alcohol Content Tables

UK Specific Gravity	USA Balling	In 1 gal (5 quarts) oz	In 4.50 litres g	Probable percentage alcohol after fermentation
1.005	1.3	2¾	78	
1.010	2.5	4¾	134	0.4
1.015	3.8	7	198	1.2
1.020	5.3	9	255	2.0
1.025	6.5	11	311	2.8
1.030	7.8	13¼	375	3.6
1.035	9.0	15½	438	4.3
1.040	9.3	17½	496	5.1
1.045	11.5	19½	553	5.8
1.050	12.5	21½	608	6.5
1.055	13.8	23¾	672	7.2
1.060	15.3	25¾	729	7.9
1.065	16.6	27¾	785	8.6
1.070	17.5	30	849	9.3
1.075	18.5	32	908	10.0
1.080	19.8	34½	979	10.6
1.085	20.8	36½	1035	11.3
1.090	22.0	38½	1092	12.0
1.095	23.0	40¾	1153	12.7
1.100	24.2	42¾	1210	13.4
1.105	25.3	44¾	1266	14.2
1.110	26.4	47	1330	14.9
1.115	27.5	49	1387	15.6
1.120	28.5	51¼	1450	16.3
1.125	29.6	53¼	1507	17.1
1.130	30.7	55½	1570	17.8

Note: 2 lb sugar occupies 1 pint of volume
      1 kg sugar occupies 620 ml of volume
      8 cups sugar occupies 1¼ pints of volume
Specific gravity figures are for liquids at 59°F/15°C
   at 68°F/20°C add 1 to the last figure
   at 77°F/25°C add 2
   at 86°F/30°C add 3½
   at 95°F/35°C add 5

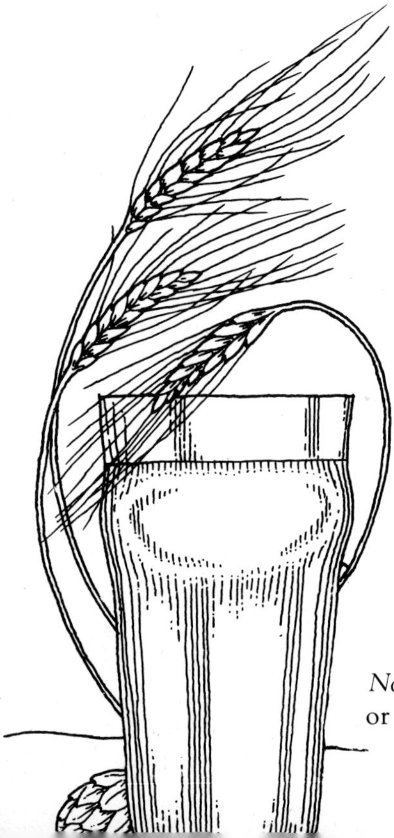

Note: Metric and Imperial conversions are *not* exact. Use one
or the other when making the recipes—never mix them.

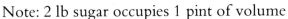

180

Useful Weights, Measures & Temperatures

	Fahrenheit	Centigrade		Imperial & USA	Metric
Freezing	32	0		¼ oz	7 g
Serve sparkling wine and cold cups	43	6		½ oz	15 g
Serve white and rosé wines	48	9		¾ oz	20 g
Serve sherry-type wines and meads	50	10		1 oz	25 g
Store wines, beers and ciders	54	12		2 oz	50 g
Ferment white wines, ciders and light ales	59	15		3 oz	75 g
Ferment and serve bitter beers and stouts	64	17.5		4 oz	115 g
Ferment red and all strong wines and ales	68	20		8 oz	225 g
Serve red wines and liqueurs				10 oz	300 g
Prepare yeast starter bottle	74	23.5		12 oz	350 g
Fermentation likely to stop	90	32		16 oz (1 lb)	450 g
Pasteurize vinegars	122	50		2 lb 3¼ oz	1 kg
Serve mulled wines	140	60			
Mash brown ales and stouts	145/149	63/65			
Mash bitter beers and strong ales	150/153	65.5/67			
Heat treatment for red fruits	176	80			
Boiling	212	100			

Imperial	Metric	USA
¼ tsp	1.25 ml	¼ tsp
½ tsp	2.5 ml	½ tsp
1 tsp	5 ml	1 tsp
1 tbsp	15 ml	1 tbsp
½ pint (10 fl oz)	300 ml	1 cup (8 fl oz)
1 pint (20 fl oz)	550 ml	1 pint (16 fl oz)
1 gal (160 fl oz)	4.5 litres	1 gal (128 fl oz)

1 Imperial gal = 6 standard bottles (wines)

= 8 pint bottles (beer)

Index